LANCELOT ANDREWES

1555–1626

A PERENNIAL PREACHER IN THE POST-REFORMATION ENGLISH CHURCH

BY

MARIANNE DORMAN

ICENI
BooKS

Lancelot Andrewes (1555-1626): A Perennial Preacher in the Post-Reformation English Church

Published by Fenestra Books™
610 East Delano Street, Suite 104, Tucson, Arizona 85705 U.S.A.
www.fenestrabooks.com

International Standard Book Number: 1-58736-341-0
Library of Congress Control Number: 2004106421

AD MAIOREM DEI GLORIAM

IN MEMORY OF RALPH

 Laid to rest on St. Birinus' Day, September 4, 2003.
Rest in peace and joy.

This is the last and great feast indeed, when all destroyers
and all destruction will cease and come to an end for evermore, and we hear that joyful voice, Transi in gaudium
Domini, "Passover into the joy of the Lord," the joys of
Heaven, joy not mingled with any leaven as this world's
joy is, but pure and entire; not transient as that of this
world, and ever flitting and forsaking us then soonest
when we think we have best hold of them, but permanent
and abiding still. A Passover that will never be passed
over, but last and continue as feast to all eternity.

—from Andrewes' Easter Day Sermon for 1612

PREFACE

On the third of November, 2005 we shall celebrate the four-hundredth year of Lancelot Andrewes' consecration as a bishop in the Church of God at the hands of Richard Bancroft, archbishop of Canterbury in St. Paul's Cathedral, London. He was assisted by the bishop of London, Dr. Vaughan, and the bishops of Norwich, Dr. Jegon, Gloucester, Dr. Ravis, and Rochester, Dr. Barlow. His consecration occurred just two days before the discovery of Guy Fawkes' plot to blow up parliament at its opening session, at which Andrewes would have been present as a member of the House of Lords.

His life as a bishop spanned almost the length of the reign of James I, who had appointed him to the see of Chichester. Almost immediately he became a regular preacher at Court for this monarch, as he had been for Elizabeth I. It would seem that he became the king's favorite preacher for the major Christian festivals: Christmas, Easter, and Pentecost. Indeed, James had some of Andrewes' sermons published shortly after hearing them in order to study them closer.

To celebrate this occasion I have put together this book, containing a cross section of doctrinal and religious themes from Andrewes' sermons for reading and reflection. Hopefully they will send the reader to the complete sermons, now available even in cyber space. At a time when various parts of the Church are questioning aspects of the Catholic or Orthodox faith and Christian morality as handed down by the Church Fathers, Andrewes' sermons will help us to appreciate the importance of being true to the faith of our Fathers in an age where there is little morality and concern for others. Perhaps this book will also enable the reader to discover Lancelot Andrewes as one of the greatest preachers and teachers in the Post-Reformation Church in England.

Finally, my thanks to the Principal, Fellows, and Scholars of Jesus College, Oxford for permission to reproduce the College's portrait of Lancelot Andrewes.

Marianne Dorman
St. Cyril of Jerusalem, March 18, 2004

CONTENTS

INTRODUCTION

Unto you therefore that be rich be it spoken;
hear your charge. I pray you. There is no
avoiding, you must needs seal this fruit of
well-doing, you must needs do it.
For having wealth and wherewithal to "do good,"
if you do it not, imprimis, talk not of faith, for
you have no faith in you; if you have wherewith
to shew it and shew it not, St. James saith
you have none to shew. Nor tell me not of your
religion, there is no religion in you; "pure religion
is this," as to very good purpose was shewed
yesterday, "To visit the fatherless and widows,"
and you never learned other religion of us.[1]

I have purposely called this book *Lancelot Andrewes, A Perennial Preacher* as I believe the themes in this book are just as relevant today as they were when Andrewes preached on them. Even in his day, over four hundred years ago, Andrewes thought that many of his contemporaries had forsaken Christian values and the importance of a right relationship with God. What would he say about our world today? Moreover, he believed many of his contemporaries had disregarded the Church's traditional practices and beliefs, as evident in this extract from his Ash Wednesday sermon from 1621/2:

---

1. Andrewes, L. *The Works of Lancelot Andrewes*, 11 vols. (Library of Anglo-Catholic Theology, J. H. Parker, Oxford, 1841-1854); afterwards referred to as Andrewes, Vol. 5, p. 36.

Every man, so we would have it, to be left to himself for prayer, fasting, Sacrament, nay for religion too now and all. For God's sake, let it not be so, let us not be left altogether to ourselves, no, not in prayer! Private prayer doth well; but let us be ordered to come to Church, and do it there, Pharisees, Publicans, Peter and John, and all; let us have our days appointed and our hours set for it.... The like say I for the Sacrament; let us have a *cum* when to come to, that too: and so for fasting; fast privately in God's name, but, hear you, let not the Church trust to that. Nor she hath not held it wisdom so to do; but as in both them, prayer and the Sacrament, so in this holds us to our order of days and times established.[2]

So have things changed? No, not all. What subjects would this prelate preach on at the beginning of the twenty-first century? I suspect he would preach in a similar vein, and so the chapters of this book all have a "perennial" appeal, as I believe the respective chapters will always be an integral part of the Christian faith for those who take this seriously, as urged by Andrewes. For example, "The Perennial Bethlehem" is not only about welcoming the Christ into our hearts at Christmas but also in the Sacrament. For Andrewes, to receive Christ's body at the Eucharist is the most wonderful and important thing we do during our earthly pilgrimage. Never are we as close to him than at that moment. "The Perennial Spring" celebrates Easter, the linchpin of the Christian faith. "If Christ be not risen then is our preaching vain, and your faith is also in vain." (1 Cor. 15:14).

Another similarity between Andrewes' time and ours is the difficult situation facing the Church. Andrewes lived in the early stages of the Post-Reformation Church in England, which was still in the process of finding her true expression. With his emphasis on upholding the Faith as taught by the Fathers and only disregarding those practices and beliefs that were contrary to that, he helped to give the English Church a healthy balance between old Catholicism and reform. As I write, the English Church is now the Mother Church of a worldwide Anglican Communion, now facing another crisis, this time over moral and doctrinal issues. Hence "The Peren-

---

2.   Ibid., Vol. 1. p. 393.

nial Path" outlines Andrewes' call for holiness and wholeness in our Christian living. This can only be achieved through grace when we acknowledge our sins, as seen in "The Perennial Repentance." If we have trouble in confessing our sins then "The Perennial Cross" should help to put this in the right perspective for us. Another helpful aid is our praise to God. This, Andrewes maintained, should never be far from our lips, as expressed in "The Perennial Gloria."

As set out in the Catechism, the purpose for our lives is to love God and to enjoy him forever. That love and enjoyment, for Andrewes, is especially shown in our worship at the Eucharist. Here we are joined with the whole company of Heaven in rendering our thanks for the sacrifice of Calvary and for Our Blessed Saviour's institution of the Eucharist. Here we receive that precious life of Christ, as set out in "The Perennial Nourishment." Included in worship for Andrewes was our own prayerful life, as illustrated in "The Perennial Praying." Nothing, but nothing, can be achieved without the Holy Spirit. Even all our festivals would not be if it were not for the Spirit always at work. So in "The Perennial Power" we discover Andrewes' devotion to the Holy Spirit, which is regenerating, renewing, and rejuvenating every aspect of creation, including us.

Thus, for Andrewes, all our time and talent is consecrated to God for his glory, and for him to use as he pleases.

AN OUTLINE OF THE LIFE OF LANCELOT ANDREWES

1555 — Born and baptized in the parish of All Hallows', Barking, London

1563 — Attended the Coopers' Free School at Radcliffe under the headship of Mr. Ward

1565 — Attended the Merchant Taylors' School in London under the headship of Richard Mulcaster

1571 — Went to Pembroke Hall, Cambridge after winning one of the newly endowed Greek scholarships by Dr. Thomas Watts, archdeacon of Middlesex. Dr. Young, who became bishop of Rochester in 1578, was the Principal

1575 — Obtained his B.A. and was elected a Fellow of Pembroke

1578 — Received his M.A. and was appointed Catechist of Pembroke. Began his catechetical lectures in the chapel

1580 — Ordained on St. Barnabas' day in the chapel of William Chaderton, bishop of Chester, and by him. Appointed junior treasurer of Pembroke

1581 — Appointed senior treasurer of Pembroke

1585 — Received his B. D.; thesis *De Usuris*

1586 — Appointed a chaplain to Elizabeth I

1588 — Received his D. D.—thesis *Of the Right of Tithes*. On receiving his doctorate, preached a sermon to the clergy on sacrilege: *Concio ad Clerum pro gradu Doctoris*

— Appointed a chaplain to the Earl of Huntingdon, who, as president of the North, took Andrewes with him on his trips to confer with Roman Catholics. Isaacson tells us he converted some

— On Easter Wednesday, preached the Spital Sermon at St. Mary's Hospital, London. This sermon appealed to the affluent of London to look after the poor. There will never be a Dives in Heaven until he has embraced a Lazarus here on earth

1589 — Elected principal of Pembroke

— Through the patronage of Walsingham, obtained the prebendary of St. Pancras at St. Paul's Cathedral, with its ancient duty of Confessor. Made Vicar of St. Giles', Cripplegate, London, a parish with a diverse population where the poor rubbed with gentry, artists, and writers

1590 — Began his lectures in term time on Genesis in St. Paul's Cathedral

1591 — Met with separatists in prison (such as Udall, Greenwood, and Barrow) to try and show them the error of their ways

1592 — Published series of sermons on the temptations of Christ as *The Wonderfull Combat*

1595 — Reinterpreted the Lambeth Articles in a more Catholic light. One of the few times Andrewes commented publicly on doctrine

1597 — Appointed a prebendary of Westminster Abbey. Resumed his Genesis lectures in St. Giles', Cripplegate, London

1601 — Appointed dean of Westminster Abbey

1603 — As dean, participated in the funeral of Elizabeth and the coronation of James I

1604 — Attended Hampton Court Conference and was appointed chairman of the translation of the first twelve books of the bible, i.e. from Genesis to 2 Kings

1605 — Offered the see of Chichester by James I and was consecrated two days before the discovery of Guy Fawkes' plot on the fifth of November by Archbishop Bancroft, assisted by the bishop of London, Dr. Vaughan, the bishop of Norwich, Dr. Jegon, the bishop of Gloucester, Dr. Ravis, and the bishop of Rochester, Dr. Barlow

— On Christmas Day, delivered his first sermon at a major festival before James I. After this he preached practically every year at the major Christian festivals until his death

1608 — Wrote *Tortura Torti*

1609 — Translated to Ely

1610 — Wrote *Responsio ad Apologiam Cardinalis Bellarmini*

1611 — Appointed one of the first governors of the Charterhouse founded by Thomas Sutton with a royal charter

— Published *Scala Coeli*, a series of lectures on prayer and the Lord's Prayer.

1616 — Made a member of the Privy Council

1618 — Made dean of the Royal Court

— Wrote his *Two Letters to Cardinal Perron*

— Corresponded with Pierre du Moulin, the French Calvinist, over episcopacy

1619 — Translated to Winchester

1625 — Participated in the enthronement of Charles I; carried the golden plate for Communion

— Charles sought his advice on the articles of Dordt

1626 — His death. "At four o'clock in the morning on 25th September this great light was extinguished." He was buried in St. Mary Ovaries, Southwark (now the Cathedral)

— The publication of the *Ninety-six Sermons* and *Opuscula quædam posthuma*

— The first publication of his catechetical lectures at Pembroke

— The first publication of *Institutiones Piæ*, a manual on how to pray based on Andrewes' papers and arranged by his amanuensis, Henry Issacson

1631 — The second edition of *The Ninety-six Sermons*

1634 — The third edition of these sermons

1641 — The fourth edition of these sermons

1642 — *The Morall Law Expounded* published

1647 — The publication of *Of Episcopacy*. This was a collection of Andrewes' answers to Peter de Moulin's letters on episcopacy

1648 — The first publication of his private prayer book by Richard Drake, as *Private Devotions*

— *A Manual for Direction of the Sick* published, based on the manual Andrewes used "in his ordinary Visitation of the Sick" at St. Giles

1653 — The publication of *A Learned Discourse of Ceremonies; retained and used in the Christian Churches*

1657 — The publication of the Genesis lectures and sermons given at St. Giles' Cripplegate as *Apospasmatia Sacra*

1675 — The publication of Greek and Latin versions of Andrewes' *Private Devotions*

1841-54— The publication of Andrewes' major works in eleven volumes by The Library of Anglo-Catholic Theology

1900 — A stained glass window depicting Andrewes preaching before James I was placed in the Hall at the Merchant Taylors' School

1919 — Andrewes' tomb was moved to the south side of the sanctuary in Southwark Cathedral and placed under a canopy designed by C. R. Bloomfield in the Jacobean style. His effigy, by Gerard Jansen, shows him in ruff and rochet with his mantle as prelate of the Most Noble Order of the Garter

CHAPTER ONE
THE PERENNIAL PREACHER

All that we can desire is for us to be with Him,
with God, and He to be with us; and we from Him,
or He from us, never to be parted.[3]

Lancelot Andrewes is well known as the most popular preacher at the Court of James I, but long before then he was a regular preacher at the Court of Elizabeth I, in his parish church of St. Giles, Cripplegate, London, and in Cambridge—where he was first Catechist and eventually master of Pembroke Hall. Not all his sermons have survived, but enough have for us to ascertain that he was one of the finest preachers of the Post-Reformation Church in England.

Andrewes has been for many people during his own day and afterwards (such as Thomas Eliot) a beacon to guide souls in the way of truth and life in the Resurrected and Glorified Lord. The faith he expounded was the Catholic faith as taught by the Fathers, which he believed was a sure way to Heaven. The Christian faith, as explained by Andrewes, is "one Canon given of God, two testaments, three symbols, the four first councils, five centuries and the series of Fathers therein."[4] Not to believe this faith, in Andrewes' opinion, excluded one from eternal salvation.

Eliot referred to Andrewes as "the first great preacher of the English Catholic Church," who he believed always spoke as "a man

---

3.   Ibid., p. 145.
4.   Ibid., Vol. 8, p. 90; Vol. 9, p. 26.

who had a formed visible Church behind him."[5] In his 1607 Nativity sermon Andrewes defended this Catholic faith against the "false conceit" that had crept "into the minds of men, to think points of religion that be manifest to be certain petty points scarce worth the hearing." For Andrewes those aspects we had to believe as Christians had been made "plain," and those not "plain" were "not necessary." Yet many of his day seemed to dispute this. "We see...how men languish about some points, which they would have thought to be great; and great controversies there be, and great books of controversies about them." Hence he pleaded for the end of controversy over essential Christian doctrine. "I hope there will be no more question or controversy...than there is of the mystery itself and the greatness of it." After all, the Faith is a "mystery," and therefore above the cavilling and contention of men, whilst the "great mystery" is God Himself, who chose to manifest himself in the flesh, not only in the "cratch" but also "on the cross." These events were certainly not matters for controversy![6]

In his sermons, as he had in his *Preces Privatæ*, Andrewes utilized a vast selection of sources. Hardly a book in the Bible was not quoted as some stage, while the Eastern and Western Fathers such as John Chrysostom, Gregory of Nyssa, Basil, Gregory Nanzianen, Irenaeus, Tertullian, Augustine, Jerome, Gregory the Great, and Bernard are quoted constantly. In one Pentecostal sermon he paid a great tribute to the Fathers when he described their writings as "lights of the Church, in whom the scent of this ointment was fresh, and the temper true."[7] He also quoted from the classical writers of ancient Greece and Rome, such as Euripides, Cicero, and Seneca, in order to contrast the pagan philosophical interpretations of life to Christ's. Hence these pagan writers "provoke Christian men to emulation, by showing them their own blindness in matter of knowledge, that see not so much as the heathen did by light of nature; or their slackness in matter of conversation, that cannot be got so far forward by God's law as the poor pagan can by his philosophy."[8]

---

5. T. S. Eliot, *For Lancelot Andrewes:Essays on Style and Order* (1928), p. 18.
6. Andrewes, Vol. 1, pp. 35-6.
7. Ibid.,Vol. 3, p. 287.
8. Ibid., Vol. 5, p. 62.

Like Augustine, many of Andrewes' sermons were "cut and paste" jobs from the Scriptures. Andrewes also often intertwined the Old and New testaments with his spiritual approach. For example, in his sermon for Christmas Day, 1613, he took as his text St. John's reference of Abraham's rejoicing in seeing "My day"(John 8:56). To illustrate how we "have Abraham for our example," Andrewes ventured to the valley of Mamre, as recorded in Genesis 18, and related how Abraham saw the birth of Christ just as clearly as the shepherds did. "But this day he saw at Mamre. Then was Christ in Person there, one of the Three; then made Abraham the confession we before spoke of."9

The Christmas joy that Abraham experienced was compared with "the joy of Job's Easter." Yet, long before Job (as recorded in Gen. 18), Abraham had indeed acknowledged his need of a Redeemer, as in when he "complains" that "I am but dust and ashes" and refers to God as "Judge of the world." This thus explained why Abraham "should desire to see this day; [and] why, but for this day Abraham had been but ashes of the furnace."10

In explaining how Abraham could see this day, Andrewes took St. Paul's interpretation of man as both a physical and spiritual being. For the latter he needs "the light of faith." It was by this means that Abraham was able to see Christ as clearly as the shepherds visibly saw the baby Jesus.11

In our understanding of God and man, Andrewes acknowledged the place of nature and reason as well as the Scriptures. He especially focused on this approach in his catechist lectures at Cambridge. Here he argued that the natural world teaches us much about God, but we nevertheless must also seek for knowledge greater than own "natural knowledge," otherwise "[we] will come to more grossness and absurdities, than the very beasts." That "higher knowledge" is given to us by God through grace, whereby we also obtain "faith...[and] eternal life." This is also true about reason. "True reason [is] a help to faith and faith to it.... When we have yielded ourselves to belief" it is strengthened "by reason." Yet we must always remember that faith, although imperfect, is a higher

---

9.   Ibid., Vol. 1, pp. 118 - 9, 128 - 9.
10.   Ibid., pp. 123 - 4.
11.   Ibid., p. 128.

teacher than reason. "Though faith be an imperfect way, and we imperfect, yet may we walk in it. We are therefore to pray to God, that by the inspiration of His Spirit, He would keep us in this way."[12] Thus to know God and ourselves, and the relationship between the two, it was essential for us to use every gift God has given. Andrewes' sermons indeed taught that all of life is hallowed and sacramental.

Andrewes' sermons, in the words of Eliot again, "rank with the finest English prose of their time." That prose was a style that endeared itself to his auditors and clearly endeared itself to the process of remembering and recalling. For this purpose the sermon was divided into various parts. The first outlined the working and manifestation of the Divine, the second detailed the benefits received from the Divine, and the third explicated the application of these benefits by the receiver. For example, his sermon for Christmas Day, 1610, with its text from St. Luke's gospel 2:10-11: the first part proclaimed that this very day, *hodie*, God became man—this is the good news; the second part showed that this Child is a Saviour for all mankind; the third announced that we are the recipients of this good news.

Andrewes manipulated and played on words in order to more fully expound upon his subject matter, with which he was spiritually, intellectually, and emotionally engrossed. An example of this *ars memorativa* technique is a Lenten sermon in 1594/5, with its text, "Remember Lot's wife." Recall is made easier by the sermon's constant appeal to "remember": "Remember the danger and damage...remember the folly...remember the disgrace...remember the scandal...remember the infamy...remember the judgment...[and] remember the difficulty of reclaiming to good" by the example of Lot's wife. Therefore, "Remember we make not light account of the Angel's *serva animam tuam*...remember, we be not weary to go whither God would have us...remember, we slack not our pace... remember we leave not our hearts behind us, but that we take that with us" as we continue on that journey to Sion. What we do now determines our future—that is, our eternal salvation.[13]

---

12.   L. Andrewes, *The Moral Law Expounded*, (London, 1642), pp. 23 -4.
13.   Andrewes, Vol. 2, pp. 73-6.

His Good Friday sermon for 1597 is another example of how Andrewes used words, what Eliot referred to as "squeezing and squeezing the word until it yields a full juice of meaning which we should never have supposed any word to possess."[14] The words that Andrewes concentrated on are "die/death," "pierce/piercing," and "heart/hart," as he wanted his auditors to not only view the Crucifixion but also to feel Christ's pain through *piercing*. Beginning with a basic quotation from Isaiah ("Die he will..."), he takes the word "die" as a command in the following sentences, each one building in intensity in order to describe the kind of death Christ faced. Thus we read:

> Die—but what death? a natural or violent? Daniel tells us He shall die, not a natural, but a violent death. But many are slain after many sorts, and [many] kinds there be of violent deaths. The psalmist...describes it thus: "they pierced My hands and My feet," which is only proper to the death of the cross. Die, and be slain, and be crucified.

Christ's death was not normal; it was especially violent. Not only were His hands and feet pierced—which was normal—but also his heart, which made it extraordinary. Thus everything climaxes in this piercing of the heart.[15]

In his application of "pierce/piercing" and "heart/hart" Andrewes intensified their meaning by using them over and over again in a slightly different context. Thus he weaved throughout his sermon that Christ's "piercing of the heart" is the fulfilment of the prophecy "And they will look upon Me Whom they have pierced." Christ is then compared "to the morning hart." Just as the *hart* is hounded "all his life long" until his end, so Christ "this day brought to His end...and stricken and pierced through side, heart, and all."[16] This "piercing" came from the "spear-point which pierced, and went through, His very heart itself; for of that wound, of the wound in His heart, is this spoken.... So that we extend this piercing of Christ farther than to the visible gash in His side, even to a piercing

---

14. Eliot, *op. cit.*, pp. 24 - 5.
15. Andrewes, Vol. 2, p. 121.
16. Ibid., pp. 119 - 20.

of another nature, whereby not His heart only was stabbed, but His very spirit wounded too."[17]

The *hart* having being slain by the "spear-point," Andrewes continued his theme of piercing the heart by redirecting *heart* and *hart*, and *pierce* and *piercing* to his listeners:

> Yes, Christ Himself, is pierced as He is, invites us to it…"Look and be pierced," yet that it might be "that with looking on Him we might be pricked in our hearts," and have it enter past the skin…and pierce that in you that was the cause of Christ's piercing upon Him and "…look and be pierced with love of Him" who so loved you, that He gave Himself in this sort to be pierced for you.[18]

Andrewes was also very much a metaphysical preacher. For example, in his 1615 Nativity sermon he wanted to convey the conceit of greatness in littleness. To achieve this he used repetition and juxtaposition, dispersed among all kinds of references to *littleness*. Bethlehem is described as a "sorry poor village; scarce worth an Apostrophe"; it is "diminutively little"; it is "the very least of all." It is "'least' for the small number of the inhabitants, 'least' for the thinness and meanness of the buildings, as was seen at Christ's Birth." This *littleness* is simultaneously juxtaposed with greatness—"so great a State"; "that birth is sure too big for this place"; and "so great a birth." To contrast further the smallness of Bethlehem with the greatness of the event which happened there, Andrewes compared this with the oak and mustard trees, both of which grow to an enormous size from a minute beginning. "How huge an oak from how small an acorn! …From how little a grain of mustard seed, the very *Bethlehem minima*, 'the least of all seeds,' how large a plant! of how fair a spread!"[19]

Another reason for Andrewes' stressing "little" was that, despite the greatness of the event, it showed that God, in becoming man, unveiled his humility—a great humility in being born in such "a sorry poor village." By being *little*, Bethlehem represents the virtue of humility, "where He in great humility was found this day." To

17. Ibid., pp. 122 - 3.
18. Ibid., pp. 130 - 2.
19. Ibid., Vol. 1, pp. 157 - 9.

come to such a *little* place, only the humble will venture, such as the shepherds; and those like "the Pharisees" are "too big for Bethlehem."[20] His message is clear: only those Christians who are humble will want to come to such a little and insignificant place, but if they do, they will discover something big!

Andrewes also used imagery to great effect. In his 1623 Paschal sermon he wished to convey the unity of Good Friday and Easter Day, that Christ, in sacrificing his life for us on the cross, conquered death through his resurrection. To achieve this, Andrewes used winepress imagery, with Christ as the winepress—but "a double winepress." Firstly, he is "Himself trodden and pressed; He was the grapes and clusters Himself," and secondly, "He who was trodden on before, gets up again and does tread upon and tread down." In the former case the winepress represented "His cross and passion," and in the latter, his release from it, "in His descent and resurrection." In the first example, when grapes are trodden a liquid, a red liquid, flows: wine. In the second it is the precious Blood of Christ. To heighten the intent of Christ pouring out his blood for mankind, Andrewes represented him as that man coming "from *Bozrah* imbrued with blood, the blood of his enemies" on his way to Edom, the place "upon earth [which] comes nearest to the kingdom of darkness in hell."[21]

In the same sermon he continued with this winery imagery to teach on the sacraments. Christ "is the true Vine, and...to make wine of Him, He and the clusters...must be pressed." In Christ's passion this blood ran forth three times: "One, in Gethsemane that made Him sweat blood"; secondly in "Gabbatha which made the blood run forth at His head with the thorns, [and] out of His whole body with the scourges"; thirdly "at Golgotha where He was so pressed that they pressed the very soul out of His body, and out ran blood and water both." Thus from His body flowed "the twin sacraments of the Church," and for this particular sermon the emphasis is on the blood, the wine from "the true Vine," which becomes "the cup of salvation." "Red" is now identified with the wine as expressed in psalm 75, "the wine is red, it is full mixed, and He pours out of it." This wine, unlike the wine made from sour grapes

---

20.   Ibid., p. 171.
21.   Ibid., Vol. 3, pp. 61,64, 66, 70.

that was offered to Christ on the cross, is pressed from good grapes and is poured into the "cup of blessing" for our salvation.[22]

Andrewes' love of souls shone through his sermons. Thus at Christmastide Andrewes rightly emphasized salvation. For the man who has been rescued from everlasting perdition, "there is no joy in the world to the joy of a man saved; no joy so great, no news so welcome, as to one ready to perish, in case of a lost man, to hear of one [who] will save him." Moreover the very "name of a saviour" brings joy, and thus we all have "cause to be glad for the birth of this Saviour" celebrated on "*diem Meum*." On "His day" there is "joy in Heaven, joy in earth" when Love became Man, so that every man could be saved.[23]

Thus his sermons revealed the joy of being a Christian, which radiated from his belief in a God who is loving, good, beautiful, compassionate, and merciful to all of his creation. Such blessings are sustained and sanctified continually by the Spirit. However, the greatest blessing for us was when the eternal Word became flesh to restore us to our former dignity. "He is not only God for us, or God with us, but God one of us"—that was the great marvel for the early Fathers, and for Andrewes. The humility of God descending to our earthly abode and taking our frail flesh never ceased to amaze Andrewes: "He was born weak and feeble as we are, an infant of a span long, in great poverty, his parents so poor, that his mother was not worth a lamb. He was obscurely brought up, increased in age, stature, wisdome, attained by degrees to his perfection, was troubled like one of us, with hunger, thirst, weariness, weakness, weeping and heaviness." It did not stop there: he was content to die a despicable death for us, so we in turn may become the sons of God.[24]

Undoubtedly for Andrewes, the Incarnation had to be the linchpin of preaching. As he said, "There is no religion but this that teacheth to the heart."[25]The Incarnation was the manifestation of

---

22.   Ibid., pp. 70 - 3.
23.   Ibid., Vol. 1, pp. 73 -4, 118, 122, 132.
24.   Lambeth Palace Ms. 3707, afterwards referred to as Ms. 3707, pp. 171, 173.
25.   Andrewes, Vol.6, p.6.

God's love, but even before, in the womb of His holy Mother, Christ showed that love:

> From which his conceiving we may conceive His great love to us-ward. Love not only condescending to take our nature upon Him, but to take it by the same way and after the same manner that we do, by being conceived.... The womb of the Virgin...He might well have abhorred...[but] He stayed...nine months.[26]

Indeed, each Christian festival is a manifestation of God's love. For example, Andrewes described Pentecost as "the feast of love"; it is the feast of "the Holy Spirit, love itself, the essential love and love-knot of the two persons of the Godhead, Father and Son." This "love-knot" is the same which exists between God and man, and even more so "between Christ and His Church."[27]

As God expressed his love for us in his Incarnation, so must we reflect that love by loving our neighbours. Thus charity, as the second bow of Christianity, featured prominently in Andrewes' sermons and prayers. Adam sinned against God, but Cain sinned against his fellow man.[28] Love therefore is the essence of our faith, and without it everything we do is worthless. A Christian cannot love God if he does not love his neighbour, including the poor, lonely, and outcast. "It sufficeth not to say to a brother or sister that is naked and destitute of daily food, 'Depart in peace, warm your selves, fill your bellies'; but the inward compassion must shew it self outwardly, by giving them those things which are needful to the body.... Our lights must so shine before all men, that the wicked and the ungodly, by seeing our good works, may take occasion to glorifie God and be converted."[29]

Andrewes lived out what he preached. Buckeridge, in his funeral oration for him, emphasized Andrewes' charity towards those less fortunate than himself by stressing that he regularly invited his poor parishioners and prisoners to share his dining table.

---

26. Ibid., Vol. 1., p.140
27. Ibid., Vol. 3, pp. 147 - 8.
28. L. Andrewes, *Apospasmatia Sacra* (London, 1657), Hereafter referred to as *Apos. Sacra.* p.415.
29. Ibid., p.585.

Although he himself ate very frugally, he always made sure there was plenty for his guests.[30]He acknowledged that everything he had was given to him from God, and so it had to be shared with others as Christ taught. In that funeral oration, Buckeridge preached:

> He wholly spent himself and his studies and estates in these sacrifices, in prayer and the praise of God, and compassion and works of charity, as if he had minded nothing else all his life long but this, to offer himself, his soul and body, a contrite and a broken heart, "a living sacrifice, holy and acceptable to God by Jesus Christ which is our reasonable service."[31]

Some other religious teachings Andrewes felt compelled to preach about during his life were the doctrines of grace and assurance. Predestinarians, of whom there were many in Andrewes' day, taught that the elect could not fall from grace or favor. He referred to the danger of believing "we are saved" in his Lenten sermon of 1594/5. Here Andrewes reiterated St. Paul's warning against false assurance. Those who feel anchored in *securitas* should be aware of sudden destruction. Like Lot's wife, we can reach the entry to the gates, "so near her safety," but still perish. "Remember, that near to Zoar gates there stands a salt-stone." Therefore we can never be secure of our salvation. From "youth...until...old age" we must not grow weary on the plain but continue faithfully to the end, "for if we stand still...we are [likely]...to be made a pillar." Furthermore, we must "remember the judgment that is upon them after their relapse." Thus it is imperative to "remember that we shall justify Sodom by so doing, and her frozen sin shall condemn our melting virtue." We must remember also "they in the wilfulness of their wickedness persisted till fire from Heaven consumed them." Andrewes warned how important it was for the "obdurate in sin" to repent, to be constant in virtue, and to practice "the Queen of virtues": perseverance.[32]

In other words it is possible for anyone, even after receiving grace, to fall from it. Every person is responsible for his or her actions, and a person's sins, unless repented of, sever their relation-

---

30. Andrewes, Vol. 11, p. xiii.
31. Ibid., Vol. 5, p. 288.
32. Ibid., Vol. 2 pp. 73 - 6.

ship with God. No aspect of Andrewes' preaching was more forceful than that of the consequences of sin. "Sin...will destroy us all." There is "nothing so dangerous, so deadly unto us, as is the sin in our bosom." Sin, when first committed, may seem "sweet," but after it is committed the sinner finds "that it turns to a bitter and choleric matter." Sin at first may perhaps seem "a matter of liberty," but it really is like "'a worm' which never leaves gnawing." Andrewes stressed that Christ died not only for our sins but also for us to cease from sin, so that it does not reign within us. To illustrate how difficult the latter is he quoted Augustine, who had insisted it was harder "to raise a soul from the death of sin...than to raise a dead body out of the dust of death." Thus "Mary Magdalene's resurrection in soul, from her long lying dead in sin, was a greater miracle than her brother Lazarus' resurrection" after being in the grave for four days.[33]

Thus the only assurance that Christians have of living in a state of grace is to repent and confess their sins regularly. In regards to the latter, Andrewes advocated auricular confession by indicating how valuable it is. He also pointed out how much it had been neglected, thus denying the parish priest of one aspect of his pastoral care:

> I take it to be an error...to think the fruits of repentance, and the worth of them, to be a matter any common man can skill of well enough; needs never ask St. John or St. Paul what he should do, knows what he should do as well as St. Paul or St. John either; and that it is not rather a matter wherein we need the counsel and direction of such as are professed that way. Truly it is neither the least nor the last part of our learning to be able to give answer and direction in this point. But therefore laid aside and neglected by us, because not sought after by you.[34]

As well as his sermons teaching the main Christian doctrines of creation, redemption, resurrection, and sanctification, they also conveyed other aspects of our religion. Andrewes, for instance, had much to say about worship. Important as the sermon was in the context of the Liturgy, Andrewes emphasized that his sermons—all

---

33. Ibid., Vol. 1, p. 74, Vol. 2, pp. 200, 203, Vol. 5, p.86.
34. Ibid., Vol. 1, pp. 450.

sermons—do not usurp worship but were merely a part of it. For him worship focused on the altar for the celebration of the Eucharist. He had a profound love for our Lord in his Sacrament, and so in most of his sermons he wove some teaching on and devotion towards the Blessed Sacrament. He could never stress enough how essential it is to receive this heavenly food on our earthly pilgrimage. It is "the means to re-establish 'our hearts with grace,' and to repair the decays of our spiritual strength; even 'His own flesh, the Bread of life, and His own blood, the Cup of salvation.'" This "Bread made of Himself, the true *Granum frumenti*, 'Wheat corn,' Wine made of Himself, 'the true Vine.'"[35] The Nativity sermons not only focused on the stable of Bethlehem and the altar being one, but also on our partaking of the divine life in the Sacrament:

> Now the bread which we break, is it not the partaking of the body, of the flesh, of Jesus Christ? It is surely, and by it and by nothing more are we made partakers of this blessed union...because He has so done, taken ours of us, we also ensuing His steps will participate with Him and with His flesh which He has taken of us. It is most kindly to take part with Him in that which He took part in with us, and that, to no other end, but that He might make the receiving of it by us a means whereby He might dwell in us, and we in Him. He taking our flesh, and we receiving His Spirit; by His flesh which He took of us receiving His Spirit which He imparts to us; that, as He by ours became *consors humanae naturae*, [a partaker of our human nature] so we by His might become *consortes Divinae naturae*, partakers of His divine nature.[36]

Thus the focal point of the Holy Eucharist is at that most precious moment of our union with Christ in the act of Communion itself. "Never can we more truly...say, *in Christo Jesu Domino nostro*, as when we come new from that holy action, for then He is in us, and we in Him." This Sacrament also had another significance for Andrewes—it was the *locus* of unity, or "the Sacrament of 'accord,'" manifested first by the Apostles as they broke bread with one accord. This "perfect unity" is also represented "in the many

---

35.   Ibid., p. 169.
36.   Ibid., p. 16.

grains kneaded into 'one loaf,' and the many grapes pressed into one cup; and what it represents lively, it works as effectually."[37]

With his profound love for the Blessed Sacrament, Andrewes deplored the attitude of those in his day who showed no reverence towards it and who refused to kneel to receive their Lord—or for that matter during the celebration of the Eucharist. So he deeply lamented the neglect of adoration. "Most come and go without it, no they scarce know what it is. And with how little reverence, how evil beseeming us, we use ourselves in the church." He also deplored the neglect towards the altar where "the highest and most solemn service of God" fares worse than any other. Regrettably people attended their parish church not for worship but to hear a sermon.[38]

As we can ascertain, his sermons expressed the need for reverence and honor in worship. This should be no less than what is given by "the glorious saints in heaven" who cast "their crown... before the throne and fall down," declared Andrewes. Indeed, worship "is [what] Cornelius did to Peter; he 'met him, fell down at his feet, and worshipped him.' And [what] John did to the Angel; that is, he 'fell down before his feet to worship him.'" Having in mind those who showed little outward reverence in the Church's worship, Andrewes argued that as man is a composite of body and soul, both parts must be expressed in worship to God. "The inward affection" can only be expressed by the outward action. It is never possible, Andrewes asserted, for "a man...[to] be too reverent to God." However, "we think it a great disgrace, and debasing of ourselves, if we use any bodily worship to God." Sadly, we would not be as irreverent to "come before a mean prince as we do before the King of kings, and Lord of lords, even the God of heaven and earth." Our attitude should be like "'the four-and-twenty elders [who] fell down before Him Who sat on the throne, and worshipped Him Who lives for ever, and cast their crowns before His throne.'" Thus at worship, he insisted, we should make "the 'knees to bow, and kneel before the Lord [our] Maker.' Our feet are [also] to 'come before His face; for the Lord is a great God, and a great King above all gods.'" Furthermore, "the wandering eye must learn to be 'fas-

---

37.   Ibid., Vol. 2, p. 205, Vol. 3, p. 128.
38.   Ibid., Vol. 2. p. 335, Vol. 4, pp. 374 - 5, 379 - 80.

tened on Him,' and 'the work of justice and peace.'" In other words, every part of the body is involved in worship.[39]

Those who scorn bodily acts of reverence, Andrewes warned, were in danger of losing their souls. Therefore he urged his contemporaries and us to follow the example of those "in heaven" or "under the earth." For "they in heaven 'cast down their crowns, and fall down' themselves of their own accord; and confess Him singing, as at His birth." Even those "under the earth do it too, but not *ultro*"; instead they "are thrown down, and even made His *footstool*... though sore against their wills; and confess Him too, though roaring...as it were upon the rack." We who live on earth, as in between, "partake of both." Hence the alternative was "either fall on our knees now, or be cast flat on our faces" later; it is a matter of "either confess Him *cantando*, with Saints and Angels, or *ululando*, with devils and damned spirits."[40]

Perhaps the most winning feature of Andrewes' preaching was that he so often preached as much to himself as to others. For instance, when preaching on a Christian's duty to pray daily each morning and evening, he added, "But who is that is able all the dayes of his life, night and day, to intend his business as he ought?"[41] Another example was when he preached on sin. Knowing only too well the battle against sin in his own life, he confessed in his 1614 Pentecost sermon, "And oh, the thraldom and misery the poor soul is in, that is thus held and hurried under the servitude of sin and Satan! The heathens' *pistrinum*, the Turkey galleys are nothing to it. If any have felt it he can understand me, and from the deep of his heart will cry, 'Turn our captivity, O Lord.'"[42]

"These and these sins so long lain in; these deserve to be bewailed even with tears of blood." Thus "we are all to pray to God to take from us the opportunity of sinning; so frail we are, it is no sooner offered but we are ready to embrace it—God help us."[43] And, "Best it were before we sin to say to ourselves, 'What am I

---

39.   Ibid., Vol. 5, pp. 554- 5.
40.   Ibid., Vol. 2, pp. 338 - 9.
41.   *Apos. Sacra*, p.132.
42.   Andrewes, Vol.3, p.228.
43.   Ibid., Vol.1, p.370, Vol.4, p.159.

now about to do?' If we have not done that, yet it will not be amiss after to say 'What have I done?'"[44]

As we try to listen to, as well as read, Andrewes' sermons, we become aware that he had "a grasp of the wholeness of the Christian faith and a conviction of the importance of theology."[45] He saw his role as "the conscience" to proclaim the Gospel. He never used the sermon for exciting emotion. As Eliot pointed out, all his sermons are purely contemplative. Any "emotion is wholly contained in and explained by its object." Nevertheless his sermons are rich, rich of detail and devotion, but reflecting that meticulousness that Andrewes had for everything in life. For Andrewes only the best was ever good enough for God, and as we ponder on the contents of his sermons, we sense they, like incense, were offered up to the heavenly court as an act of worship to his Creator, Redeemer, and Sanctifier.

---

44.   Ibid., Vol.1, p.339.
45.   P. Welsby, *Lancelot Andrewes* (London, 1958), p. 294.

CHAPTER TWO
THE PERENNIAL BETHLEHEM:
THE NATIVITY

O little town of Bethlehem
How still we see thee lie!
Above thy deep and dreamless sleep
The silent stars go by.
Yet in thy dark streets shineth
The everlasting light;
The hopes and fears of all the years
Are met in thee to-night.[46]

In 1620, as Bishop of Winchester, Andrewes consecrated the church of St. Mary's, Southampton, during which an offertory collection was taken, amounting to £4/12/2. Andrewes used this to have a gothic covered chalice crafted for this little church. On its cover a star was engraved—not any star, but the star of Bethlehem. In his Christmas sermon of the same year he explained its significance: "In the old Ritual of the Church" this "wise men's star" was engraved "on the cover of the canister, wherein was the Sacrament of his body...to show that now the star leads us thither, to His body there."[47]

---

46. P. Brookes, *New English Hymnal* (Canterbury Press, Norwich, 1988), p. 52.
47. Andrewes; Vol. 1, pp. 235, 247; Oman, C.C. *English Church Plate*, (London, 1957), p. 205.

In a Nativity sermon given five years earlier he had depicted this star of Bethlehem always hovering over where Jesus is, and therefore "the star does lead us to Bethlehem straight. Never stood still till it came thither, and there it stood directly over the place, as much to say as, 'Lo, there He is born.'" By this Andrewes specifically meant that wherever the Eucharist is celebrated there is Bethlehem. "Of which Bread the Church is this day the house, the true Bethlehem, and all the Bethlehem we have now left to come to for the Bread of life,—of that His life which we hope for in heaven." Thus this little town is not only the place where the Lord Jesus was born but also where he continues to be physically present, even today, Christmas Day on the altar. And wherever the Eucharist is celebrated the star will burn brightly in the heavens, beckoning all to come and find the Lord Jesus. "Where that Bread is, there is Bethlehem for ever.... There shall ever be this day a Bethlehem to go to— a house wherein there is bread, and this bread."[48]

For us, unlike for the *magi*, our Bethlehem is so very near. "And will there be Bethlehem, and so near us, and shall we not go to it? Or, shall we go to it, to the House of Bread, this Bread, and come away without it? Shall we forsake our Guide leading us to a place so much for our benefit?" After all, the star declares that it is Christ's "office to lead and to feed us" just as much as it is "our duty to be led and to be fed by Him."[49] So come! *Venite*! Let us be like the *magi* and come to the House of Bread.

> And what shall I say now, but according as St. John says, and the star, and the wise men say, "Come." And He, Whose the star is, and to Whom the wise men came, says, "Come." And let them who are disposed, "Come." And...take of the "Bread of Life, which came down from heaven" this day into Bethlehem, the house of bread.[50]

During our earthly pilgrimage, coming to our Bethlehem—the altar—is the nearest we can come to experiencing our dear Lord until we are called to "another *venite* come, unto Him in His heavenly kingdom, to which He grant we may come." There, in Heaven

---

48.   Andrewes, Vol.1, pp. 154 - 5, 174, 246.
49.   Ibid., pp. 156, 174.
50.   Ibid., pp. 247 - 8.

in never ending "joyful days," we shall gaze and gaze upon the Lamb of God.[51]

And what of the village of Bethlehem itself? What significance does it bear for us? Of course it is "the place where David himself was born. And what place more meet for the Son of David to be born." Yet, more importantly for Andrewes, this is Bethlehem Ephratah, belonging to the tribe of Judah rather than that Bethlehem belonging to the tribe of Zebulon. In comparison therefore it is a tiny "sorry, poor village, scarce worth an Apostrophe...and as little likelihood, that so great a State as the Guide of the whole world should come creeping out such a corner." Surely then it is not the place for a birth of a King; "that birth is sure too big for this place." No, said Andrewes, "As little as it is," Bethlehem Ephratah was meant to become immortalised, as "no little Person shall come out of it.... One, Whose only coming forth of it was able to make it not the least, [but] the greatest and most famous of all the dwellings of Jacob, of the whole land, no, of the whole world."

Indeed, Christ's birth in this little village resembles the small acorn, which, when it germinates, grows into a huge oak; or "a grain of mustard-seed, the very *Bethlehem minima*, 'the least of all seeds,' how large a plant! of how fair a spread! and that in a little time." The littleness of the village also reflects the virtues of "lowliness and humility," and so this is the "natural birth place" for Christ to be born, as "humility is His place."[52]

> And O thou little Bethlehem, and O thou little Bethlemite, how do you both, both place and person, confound the haughtiness of many that yet would be called Christians, and even near Christ Himself. There is in both of you, if it were well taken to heart, enough to prick the swelling, and let out the apostumed matter of pride many of us, whose look, gesture, gait and swelling words of vanity are too big for Bethlehem.[53]

Significantly, Bethlehem Ephratah means "fruitfulness," as compared to Bethlehem in Zebulon, which denotes barrenness. "The

---

51.   Ibid., pp. 174, 248.
52.   Ibid., pp. 157-9, 238.
53.   Ibid., p. 161.

next station is to the next virtue, and that is Ephratah, 'fruitfulness'...for He has brought forth...'a lasting seed'; the fruit whereof to this day 'shakes like Libanus, and as the green grass covers all the earth'.... [Thus] to humility to add fruitfulness."

Fruitfulness was a term constantly used by Andrewes, as he strongly believed that Christians must express their faith outwardly, in acts of charity as well as by mortification. Thus there was little good in simply talking about one's religion; it had to be lived out. He explained:

> By this I mean plenteousness in all good works. Else it is not Ephratah...not right repentance unless it be Ephratah, "bring forth fruits of repentance"; nor faith, "without the work of faith"; nor love, "without the labour of love"; nor any other virtue without her Ephratah.... Fruitful then...not the fruit of the lips, a few good words "but the precious fruit of the earth," as St. James calls it—*lehem*, "good bread," that fruit. Such fruit as St. Paul carried to the poor saints at Jerusalem, "alms and offerings".... Now if we could bring these together...straight we cease to be little; we begin to talk of merit and worth, and I [know] not what. So our lives must imitate the tiny hamlet of Bethlehem Ephratah.[54]

The meaning of Bethlehem is also significant. "*Beth* is a house, *lehem* bread, and *Ephratah* is plenty.... Bethlehem then sure a fit place for...[Him] to be born in." Thus there is "no more proper [place] for Him Who is 'the living Bread that came down from heaven,' to give life to the world.... His house is the house of bread, inasmuch as He Himself is Bread; that in the house or out of it— wheresoever He is, there is Bethlehem."[55]

Andrewes, in elaborating on Christ as the Bread of Life and Bethlehem as the House of Bread, compared Christ's nourishing of His people with that of Moses and the provisions he made for the Israelites in Egypt and in their wanderings in the desert.

> You may see all this represented in the shadows of the Old Testament...

---

54. Ibid., pp. 171 -2.
55. Ibid., p. 168.

[Firstly] Moses, when he came to lead the people, found them…
"scattered over all the land of Egypt, to seek stubble for brick," to
build a city that sought the ruin of them all. Our case right the
very pattern of it; when our Guide finds us wandering in vanity,
picking up straws, things that will not profit us; "seeking death in
the error of our life," till we be so happy as to light into His guiding.

Secondly, Moses was not only "a guide for the way"; but also
when enemies came forth against them, "a captain for the war."
Christ was so too, and far beyond Moses. For He made us way
with laying down of His life. So did neither Moses nor Joshua.
Would die for it, but He would open us a passage to the place He
undertook to bring us to. Was *Dux*, a Guide, in His life; *Dux*, a
Captain, in His death.

Thirdly, Moses when they fainted by the way obtained in their
hunger manna "from Heaven," and in their thirst "water out of
the rock for them." Christ is Himself the "true Manna"; Christ,
the spiritual Rock. Whom He leads He feeds; carries Bethlehem
about Him.[56]

Yet for Andrewes, Bethlehem was never truly named until the
day of Christ's birth.

And in this respect it may well be said, Bethlehem was never
Bethlehem right, had never the name truly till this day this birth,
this Bread was born and brought forth there. Before it was the
house of bread, but of the bread that perishes; but [now] of the
'Bread that endures to everlasting life.'

Thus the symbolism of Bethlehem was the ordaining of the
Sacrament "to re-establish 'our hearts with grace,' and to repair the
decays of our spiritual strength; even 'His own flesh, the Bread of
life,' and 'His own blood, the Cup of salvation.' Bread made of Himself, the true *Granum frumenti.*"[57]

---

56. Ibid., pp. 168–9.
57. Ibid., p. 170.

There is another similarity between Bethlehem—with its cratch in a cave—and the altar upon which are the elements of bread and wine:

> For Christ in the Sacrament is not altogether unlike Christ in the cratch. To the cratch we may well like the husk or outward symbols of it. Outwardly it seems little worth, but it is rich of contents, as was the crib this day with Christ in it. For what are they, but weak and poor elements of themselves? yet in them find we Christ. Even as they did this day in the beasts' crib the food of angels; which very food our signs both represent, and present unto us.[58]

For the sake of what Bethlehem signifies, Andrewes pleaded that we give due honor to it, as He Who came out of it will bring us to eternity:

> For little Bethlehem's sake... love the virtue that is like it, and for the virtue's sake to honour it. Honour it, there is a star over it, there is a Saviour in it. Honour it for That which comes out of it, for the fruit it yields. More good comes forth out of that poor town, says the prophet...than from all the great and glorious cities in the world.... Bethlehem..."gives us our introduction to paradise."[59]

> O *holy Child of Bethlehem,*
> *Descend to us, we pray;*
> *Cast out our sins, and enter in,*
> *Be born in us today.*[60]

---

58. Ibid., p.213.
59. Ibid., p. 162.
60. Brookes, op.cit, p.53.

CHAPTER THREE
THE PERENNIAL STAR:
THE MAGI'S JOURNEY

A cold coming we had of it.
Just the worst time of the year
For a journey, and such a long journey:
The ways deep and the weather sharp,
The very dead of winter.[61]

The star of Christmas has become associated with a particular journey and visit made by eastern kings who travelled a long distance over hazardous terrain and dangerous territory to reach the little village of Bethlehem, outside of Jerusalem. These visitors have become known as the *magi*, or the wise men, and they and their trip have been immortalised by Thomas Eliot[62] in the first of his Ariel Poems, titled *Journey of the Magi*. The opening five lines are those above, a direct quote from Andrewes' Nativity sermon for 1622.[63]

---

61. Andrewes, Vol. 1, p. 257. It is also the first verse of T. S. Eliot's poem *The Journey of the Magi*. T. S. Eliot, *Selected Poems* (London, 1980), pp. 97 - 8.
62. It was probably Andrewes' sermons which had the greatest influence upon Eliot's conversion to Christianity, and to a particular strain, English Catholicism.
63. Andrewes' sermons bear resemblance to the homilies given by St. John Chrysostom in the equivalent verses from St. Matthew. St. Chrysostom in *The Nicene and Post-Nicene Fathers*, 1st series, Vol. 10 (Edinburgh, 1991), pp. 36. - 43).

Andrewes unfolded in his sermon the dangers the *magi* faced: "Their journey...[was] exceeding dangerous, as lying through the midst of the 'black tents of Kedar,' a nation of thieves and cut-throats; to pass over the hills of robbers, infamous then, and infamous to this day."[64]

As Eliot continued his poem he expressed these dangers as:

And the camels galled, sore-footed, refractory,
Lying down in the melting snow.
There were times we regretted
The summer palaces on slopes, the terraces,
And the silken girls bringing sherbet.
Then the camel men cursing and grumbling
And running away, and wanting their liquor and women,
And the night-fires going out, and the lack of shelters,
And the cities hostile and the towns unfriendly
And the villagers dirty and charging high prices:
A hard time we had of it.
At the end we preferred to travel all night,
Sleeping in snatches,
With the voices singing in our ears, saying
That this was all folly.

Eliot's *Journey of the Magi* is worth reflecting upon time and time again for its own worth, as well as its portrayal of the message of Andrewes' two sermons on the *magi*: that once we set out to find Christ that journey will often be "hard and bitter"; there will be many "deaths" along the road before we finally embrace Christ. Yet that finding does not bring satisfaction but a disturbing uneasiness. The cross already hovers over the cratch. That is the nature of the pilgrimage to our native home.

Andrewes' sermons, however, concentrate not only on the *magi's* journey but also upon the star that sparked the journey. The star was a new light that illuminated the darkened and distant horizon, manifesting that some great happening had transpired. "A new light kindles in heaven, a star never seen before. The world could not but look up at it, and ask what it meant... 'and [so] the news of it [went] to the utmost parts of the earth.'"[65] Such a star alerted and

---

64. Andrewes, Vol.1, p. 257.
65. Ibid., p. 234.

beckoned the learned and princely *magi*, who, as they were well versed in astrology, recognized the extraordinary significance of such an appearance. "This is their star, their guide; a guide apt and proper for them who knew the stars, for them who were learned." The appearance for Andrewes of such a star was also a pointer for those who seek truth in any "human learning," as they will eventually discover that it leads to the ultimate Truth. No truth "thwarts any truth in Divinity, but sorts well with it and serves it, and all to honour Him Who says of Himself *Ego sum Veritas*, 'I am the Truth.'"[66]

So the *magi* undertook to discover Truth, which they found wrapped in swaddling clothes. But, as they were learned men, their journey revealed that Christ's birth, humble as it was, was not only for the simple but also for the learned. Thus "Christ is not only for russet cloaks, shepherds and such…but even the grandees, great states such as these, *venerunt*, they 'came' too; and when they came were welcome to Him. For they were sent for and invited by this star, their star properly." Thus applying knowledge and learning should never be a barrier to humility. As Andrewes expressed it, "The shepherds were a sort of poor simple men altogether unlearned. But here come a troop of men of great place, high account in their country; and withal of great learned men, their name gives them for no less." Hence "wealth, worth, or wisdom shall hinder none, but they may have their part in Christ's birth as well as those of low degree."[67]

Thus another important aspect of the *magi's* coming was that, unlike the shepherds, they belonged to the Gentile world, and accordingly manifested that Christ's coming was for all. In that sense they represented us at Christ's Nativity. Hence Andrewes encourages us to "look out" and see "if we can see this star. It is ours, it is the Gentiles' star. We may set our course by it, to seek and find, and worship Him as well as they."[68]

When the *magi* reached where the star hovered above the stable of Bethlehem, they instantly displayed implicit trust and faith. They did not ask "*ubi est?* Not whether He be born, but 'where He

---

66. Ibid., p. 245.
67. Ibid., pp. 234 - 5.
68. Ibid., pp. 234-5.

is born.' For born He is they are sure, by the same token they have seen His star."[69] Their faith was also shown when they reached Judæa, as they spoke openly about making such a hazardous journey to find the "king" to another king.

> They were no sooner come, but they spake of it so freely, to so many, as it came to Herod's ear and troubled him not a little that any King of the Jews should be worshipped beside himself. So then their faith is no bosom-faith, kept to themselves without saying anything of it to anybody.... The star in their hearts cast one beam out at their mouths. And though Herod who was but *Rex factus* could evil brook of *Rex natus*, must needs be offended at it, yet they were not afraid to say it.... So neither afraid of Herod, nor ashamed of Christ; but professed their errand, and cared not who knew it. This for their confessing Him boldly.[70]

Thus the *magi* by their example revealed the difference between "*fidelis*, well-grounded" faith, and "*credulus*, lightness of belief." In seeing the new star, assisted "by the light of their prophecy," they immediately believed this star herald some significant happening. They did not stand still and simply gaze at the star; but it was like the morning light drawing them, urging them and bringing them to the place where Jesus was born, and so Andrewes prompts us to see the star and to do likewise. "But by this we see, when all is done, hither we must come for our morning light." Once we "have seen His star," it is important that He sees that our star burns in us through the faith implanted by the Holy Spirit, as it did in the *magi*. "*Vidimus stellam* is as good as nothing without it." Andrewes went on to explain:

> There must be a light within the eye; else...nothing will be seen. And that must come from Him, and the enlightening of His Spirit.... He sending the light of His Spirit within into their minds, they then saw clearly, this the star, now the time, He the Child who this day was born.

---

69.   Ibid., p. 236.
70.   Ibid., p. 253.

Thus "the light of the star in their eyes, the 'word of prophecy' in their ears, the beam of His Spirit in their hearts; these three made up a full *vidimus*."[71]

Although the *magi* have come to represent us in following the star, Andrewes still asked: If we were left to our own devices to follow this new heavenly light to find the Christ-child, would we have come? And if we decided we would make the journey, would we go immediately, or would we have hesitated or even postponed it? For the *magi* there was no hesitation, despite its timing "at the worst time of the year." "They set forth this very day.... So desirous were they to come...and to be there as soon as possibly they might; broke through all these difficulties."

> It was but *vidimus, venimus*, with them; no sooner saw, but they set out presently. So as upon the first appearing of the star...it called them away, they made ready straight to begin their journey this morning. A sign they were highly conceited of His birth, believed some great matter of it, that they took all these pains, made all this haste that they might be there to worship Him with all the possible speed they could. Sorry for nothing so much as that they could not be there soon enough, with the very first, to do it even this day, the day of His birth.[72]

Even if we decided to make the journey, would it have been as swift as that of the *magi*? Not likely, thought Andrewes.

> It would have been but *veniemus* at the most. Our fashion is to see and see again before we stir a foot, specially if it be to the worship of Christ. Come such a journey at such a time? No; but fairly have put it off to the spring of the year, till the days longer, and the ways fairer, and the weather warme.r... Our Epiphany would sure have fallen in Easter-week at the soonest.[73]

The faith of the *magi* kindled by the heavenly star suggested another star for Andrewes—it is what St. Peter called the "'Day-star which rises in the heart,' that is faith, which shined and manifested

---

71. Ibid., 253, 255 - 6.
72. Ibid., pp. 233 - 4, 257.
73. Ibid., p. 258.

itself by their labour in coming, diligence in enquiring, dutying in worshipping."[74] And of course there was another star, a third star, the brightest star, "Christ Himself, 'the bright morning star,' whom both the other guide us to; the Star of this morning which makes the day the greatest day in the year."

All three stars hearken *venite adoremus*, which is what the *magi* did. They were no sooner with the Christ-child than they fell down and worshipped Him and offered their gifts. Christ invites us to "come and seek, and find and worship Him, that is do as these did."[75] However, Andrewes has doubts about our *venite adoremus*. We are full of all kinds of excuses, even though our journey to Bethlehem is so much shorter and simpler in comparison to that of the *magi*. "What excuse shall we have if we come not? If so short and so easy a way we come not, as from our chambers hither, not to be called away indeed? Shall not our *non venerunt* have an *ecce?*" No, believed Andrewes, our attitude to worship Christ is so different from that of the *magi*.[76]

Even when we do come we have no urgent desire to adore him, to bow down and give him his worth. Yet to be Christ's faithful servants, "We must learn...to ask where He is, which we full little set ourselves to do. If we stumble on Him, so it is; but for any asking we trouble not ourselves, but sit still as we say, and let nature work; and so let grace too, and so for us it will." However, Andrewes warned that "Christ has His *ubi*, His proper place where He is to be found; and if you miss of that, you miss of Him. And well may we miss, says Christ Himself."[77]

Andrewes stressed that once we have made the effort to come and have found the Babe it is imperative that we follow the example of the *magi*, who showed us that it is the doing that is the most important aspect of our faith—and which will win us Heaven in the end. Their doing was of course expressed in their worship of both body and soul when they knelt before their Lord and presented their gifts. Likewise we too must "fall down" and worship Him "with our worldly goods that may be seen and felt *offerentes*."[78]

---

74. Ibid., p.236.
75. Ibid.
76. Ibid., p. 258
77. Ibid., pp. 258 - 9.
78. Ibid., pp. 262 - 3.

Andrewes then asked:

And how shall we do that? I know not any more proper way left us, than to come to that which Himself by express order has left us, as the most special remembrance of Himself to be come to. When He came into the world, says the psalm, that is at His birth now, He said, *Ecce venio.* What then? "Sacrifice and burnt-offering You would not have, but a body have You ordained me...." By the "offering," breaking, and partaking of which "body, we are all sanctified," so many as will come to it. "For given it is, for the taking away of our sins." Nothing is more fit than at the time His body was ordained Him, and that is today, to come to the body so ordained.[79]

The star changed the live of the *magi*, as evident in the last lines of Eliot's poem:

We returned to our places, these Kingdoms,
But no longer at ease here, in the old dispensation,
With an alien people clutching their gods.
I should be glad of another death.[80]

Once having made the journey to see Christ, our lives will never be the same again either. That burning light of the star will continually impel us to know and follow the Truth.

---

79.   Ibid., p. 247.
80.   Eliot, op.cit., pp. 97 - 8.

CHAPTER FOUR
THE PERENNIAL GLORIA:
THE ANGELS

Glory be to God in the highest and peace on earth to all men.

So we all sing with great gusto at Midnight Mass at Christmas.
And why not? It is celebrating the greatest event in history.

On that most holy of all nights the heavens exploded with
amazing light. What had caused it? The birth of Christ as the
angelic hosts rejoiced in His birth. "No sooner had [the angel] delivered his message, but 'presently there was with him a whole choir
of angels,' singing, and joying and making melody, for this 'good-will
of God towards men.'" In those wee hours of the night the only
people they could tell it to were poor shepherds tending their flock
in the fields. "None were then awake...but...poor shepherds, and
to them he told it." How appropriate it was, Andrewes mused, to
tell those who tended lambs "of a strange Lamb" who would "take
away the sin of the world" and to lead them to "the Good Shepherd
who would give His life for His flock." The shepherds were also
given a sign: "you will find him wrapped in swaddling clothes, laying
in a manger." So the cratch is a sign, it "is the cradle of his love, no
less than His humility." It is thus not only "a sign" but also a "good
sign" for the poor, like the shepherds, and indeed for us all. [81]

Despite the comforting and celebratory news from the angel,
the shepherds were overcome by the dazzling, heavenly light and
became afraid. To dispel such fear, the angel's first words to the

---

81.   Andrewes, Vol. 1, pp. 64-5, 209, 215.

shepherds were ones of comfort. "Fear not!" he tells them. "'They were afraid,' and that 'sore afraid'…[so] this fear must be removed." The angel thus immediately announced, "'I bring you good news,'" which, as Andrewes indicated, means "'fear not' but be of good cheer…. Fear no ill, there is none to fear; there is no ill, no there is good towards. For good news is good, in that it represents the good itself to us before it [comes]."

Fortified by this "good cheer," the shepherds were led by this heavenly light directly to the stable, in a town "full of strangers." On finding the Babe, they followed the angels in praising "God, 'for that they had heard and seen.'"[82]

> And so on this most holy night both Heaven and earth join in praise. Heaven on high, earth beneath to take up one hymn; both in honour of His birth—both are better by it. Heaven has glory, earth peace, by means of it…. Warranted by this song, at Thy nativity, O Lord, let the heavens rejoice for the glory, let the earth be glad for the peace that come to them by it.

> And men…though they rest and come in last after both, yet they to do it as much…for God's good-will toward them which brought all this to pass in heaven and earth both; restoring men to God's favour and grace, and all by means of this Child.[83]

In analysing the Angel's message, Andrewes emphasised that the joyful anthem sung on that first Christmas night proclaimed three important messages: "glory," "peace," and "good-will." Out of these three, "goodwill" was the most important for us, as it signified the "good pleasure" God showed towards His son, and in turn to us, not only at His birth but also at His Baptism and Transfiguration.

> Glory from us to Him, peace from Him to us. From men on earth to God on high, glory; from God on high to men on earth, peace. Men I say, towards whom He is now appeased, and with whom now He well-pleased; and both, for this Child's sake here in the cratch, in Whom He is so absolutely well-pleased, as of the full-ness of His favour we all receive. God spoke it once, and twice; once at his Baptism; and again in the Holy Mount.

---

82.   Ibid., pp. 68, 197, 213.
83.   Ibid., pp.215-6.

It also showed how "well-pleased" he was with the nature of man and to take that nature Himself.

And *hoc erit signum*, this may be a sure sign that He is well-pleased with our nature, that He has in this Child taken it and united it to His own; which, if He had not been highly well-pleased, He would never have done. What greater good-will can there be than this? It passes the greatest, even that of marriage—union of nature, unity of person.... Now has God glory, now earth peace. Men are now received to favour and grace.

As we have been honored with "favour and grace" by God's "good pleasure," Andrewes suggested that we should display his "good pleasure" by giving God more praise than we had previously given. "The point of glory much mended; God more glory than before." This in turn will make "earth more at peace, if you take peace in things spiritual, matters concerning the soul."[84]

This message of "peace on earth" furthermore denoted the reunion of God and man through the holy Christ-Child. Although God had shown many favors in the past to man, none could rescue him from his fallen state. Reconciliation with God could only be accomplished when the "Godhead and manhood meet both in one." The angels thus sing "'at His Nativity of those things that came by His Nativity.' Came to heaven, to earth, to men. Glory to heaven, peace to earth, grace and favour to men.... [This] good-will to men [is] in the midst between both, compound of both." Thus:

The Child here is God and Man. God from on high, Man from the earth. To Heaven whence He is God, thither goes glory; to earth whence Man, thither peace. Then as God and Man is one Christ, and as the reasonable soul and flesh is one man; so Christ consisting of these two brings the "fullness of God's favour," the true and real cause of both; yielding them peace while here on earth, and assuring them of glory when there on high; as thither on high we trust to be delivered after our time here spent in procuring Heaven glory and earth peace.[85]

---

84. Ibid., pp. 215, 218, 228.
85. Ibid., pp. 216, 219.

The tidings of "peace on earth" is not only good news but also joyful news, as the angel advised the shepherd of the birth of a Saviour. It is the night of "*gaudium magnum*," as Andrewes called it. It is "joy" because the Lord has come; it is "great joy" as he has come to redeem mankind. And so the best joy in the world "is the joy of a man saved; no joy so great, no news so welcome, as to one ready to perish, in case of a lost man, to hear of one who will save him, [and] in danger of perishing by sickness, to hear one that will make him well again.... It is the best news he ever heard in his life. There is joy in the name of a Saviour.... We have therefore all cause to be glad for the birth of this Saviour."[86]

Not only is there joy in the coming of the Christ-Child but also hope. We are no longer "hope's prisoners," as He who "should come is come. The promised Saviour, the Saviour Which is Christ is now born.... Now there is a saving office erected, One anointed to that end, a professed Saviour to Whom all may resort.... 'There is a name under heaven' whereby we may be sure of salvation, the Name of Christ."[87]

Yet "Christ" must always be linked with "Lord," and so the next heralding by the angel called the Child "Lord": "And yet, to make our joy more full the Angel adds the third. 'A Saviour Who is Christ,' Christ the Lord...Lord of men and angels, Lord of heaven and earth, and all the hosts of them." Andrewes explained why it was necessary to add "lord":

> As He is Christ, that is, anointed, He is man only. It is His name as Man, for God cannot be anointed. But He who should save us would be more than Man; and so, more than Christ. Indeed, Christ cannot save us. He who must save us must be the Lord... [and] because He is the Lord, "endures for ever"...He forever [is]..."Author of eternal salvation" to all who depend on Him... To begin and to end; to save soul and body from bodily and ghostly enemies; from sin the root, and misery the branches; for a time and for ever; to be a Saviour and to be salvation itself; Christ the Lord is all this, and can do all this. Now then we are right, and never till now.[88]

---

86. Ibid., pp. 70, 73-4.
87. Ibid., p.77.
88. Ibid., p.78.

Andrewes goes on to enumerate additional mercies derived from this name that has placed us in a better state than where we were before the Fall:

> "Lord" goes yet further, not only to save us and set us free from danger, to deliver us from evil; but to state us in as good and better condition than we forfeited by our fall, or else though we were saved we should not save by the match. To make us then savers, and not savers only, but gainers...He does further impart also the estate annexed of this last title, even whatsoever He is Lord of Himself.[89]

In the words of Paul, as quoted by Andrewes, Christ is also the "Lord of life," meaning that he imparts life to all, while Peter called him the "Lord of glory," and thus he confers glory upon all. These two, when combined with the title "Lord of joy," mean that he makes us "lords" of "life and glory and joy." Furthermore, "He admits us with Himself into His estate of joint-purchase of heaven...that in right of it we may enter into the life, glory, and joy of our Lord, and so be saved and be savers, and more than savers every way."[90]

Thus when we combine everything the angel told the shepherds we have various combinations:

> ...natus and Servato, Servator and Christus, Christus and Dominus, Dominus and natus; "born and Saviour," "Saviour and Christ," "Christ and the Lord," "the Lord and born;" take them which way you will in combination, any of the four, then have we His two natures in one Person. In Servator, His Godhead; none but God is a Saviour. In Christus, His Manhood; God cannot be anointed, man may. In Dominus, His divine again, "the Lord from heaven." In Natus, His human nature directly, born of a woman; both ever carefully joined, and to be joined together. [91]

Obviously, stated Andrewes, this Saviour was quite distinct from those "saviours raised up of a sudden upon some occasion, to serve the turn for the present, and never heard of till they came."

---

89. Ibid., p. 79.
90. Ibid., p. 81.
91. Ibid.

Christ was "signed and sent with absolute commission and fullness of power to be the perfect and complete Saviour of all...not for a time, but for ever; not to the Jews, as did the rest, but even to all the ends of the earth." Our Saviour is also the fulfiller of all the prophets. By combining all the different roles of the past prophets such as "Aaron the Priest, Elisha the Prophet [and] Saul the King" Christ is all—Priest, Prophet and King. These offices and his kingdom will endure forever.[92]

This blessed birth as announced by the angel

> of a Saviour Which is Christ the Lord' thus furnished in every point to save us throughly, body and soul, from sin the destruction, and Satan the destroyer of both, and that both here, and for ever—this blessed and thrice blessed birth is the substance of this day's solemnity of the Angel's message, and our joy.[93]

Like the shepherds, we too are given a sign to come and "find this Child," but unlike them we do not have far to go, as Christ is close by in the Sacrament. Indeed, Andrewes drew a parallel between "Christ in the Sacrament" and in the cradle.

> To the cratch we may well like the husk or outward symbols of it. Outwardly it seems little worth but it is rich of contents, as was the crib this day with Christ in it. For what are they, but *infirma et egena elementa*, "weak and poor elements" of themselves? yet in them find we Christ. Even as they did this day in the beasts' crib the food of Angels; which very food our signs both represent, and present unto us.

Thus there is double reason to sing the angelic hymn "Glory to God in the highest and on earth, and peace to his people on earth" on Christmas Day, as we are never closer to the angels, suggested Andrewes, than just after we have received the "holy Sacrament of His blessed Body and most precious Blood." So let us proclaim joyfully this wonderful news of that first Christmas night when the heavens were filled with glorious light at the birth of our Saviour, who is ever with us on the altar in the Blessed Sacrament.[94]

---

92.   Ibid., pp. 76-7
93.   Ibid., p.81.
94.   Ibid., pp. 213-4

CHAPTER FIVE
THE PERENNIAL PREPARATION:
LENT

It is so set by the Church, the time of it,
that our Lent will end with an Easter,
the highest and most solemn feast
in the year, the memory of Christ's rising,
and the pledge of our blessed and joyful resurrection.[95]

Lent, although not quite as old as Easter in observance by the Church, from very early times has been a period of solemn preparation for the celebrating of our Lord's glorious Resurrection at Eastertide. In the early Church it was particularly associated with the training and discipline of catechumens to be received into the Church with Baptism at the Easter Vigil.

In the eight extant Ash Wednesday sermons of Andrewes, with their themes revolving around the epistle and gospel for that day, he set forth what that solemn preparation entailed, not only for the catechumens of old but especially for his contemporary Christians. He depicted Lent as that precious time given for making a reckoning of our lives and, accordingly, for making our amends by repentance—and afterwards by fasting, prayer, and almsgiving. We can "safely seek and surely find God...by the timely fruits of an undelayed repentance," and be renewed in vigour and vision, as Andrewes would say.[96]

---

95.   Ibid., p. 374.
96.   Ibid., p.320.

Put another way, Lent is the time the Church has given us to prepare our gardens for Easter blooming. Just as Andrewes portrayed the glories of Easter in spring imagery, so likewise he depicted Lenten discipline and preparation in horticultural imagery. Accordingly, in his Ash Wednesday sermons he directed us to look upon the fields, where we shall discover it is the time of planting and "men grafting and setting trees: it is the husbandry and the business of the month." "There cannot be a fitter time than the Church has set...forth" for teaching repentance, renewal, and rejuvenation. How "wonderfully fitly chosen...that this [Lenten] tree may keep time with the rest." Just as the husbandman must not defer his planting if he desires his fruits of the earth, so we must not defer repentance "but take the time while it is [the] season...[so] that the mortifying of sin might end in the rising of Christ in us."[97] Thus repentance is not something that is quickly done or lightly dispatched; it takes much toil. Neither must it be delayed. We must not be like the people in Jude (verse 12), that is, "our seeking all summer withered and dry, and beginning to shoot out a little about Michaelmas spring. Of which kind of fruit can never come."[98]

Andrewes emphasised that the Church, in her wisdom, had set apart the time of Lent to "have us seriously to entend and make it our time of turning to the Lord." Thus he would say it is "a time 'lent' us as it were by God, set us by the Church, to make our turning."[99] Andrewes could not overemphasize the importance of the *now*, "'now' at this time, it is the time that all things turn, now is the only sure part of our time. That which is past is come and gone, that which is to come may peradventure never come. Till to-morrow, till this evening, till an hour hence, we have no assurance."[100]

Therefore we too need to reflect on our sins:

> ...stay a little, turn and look back upon our sins past; it may be, if we could get ourselves to do it in kind, if set them before us and look sadly, and not glance over them apace; think of them not once, but..."think them over and over"; consider the motives, the base motives, and weigh the circumstances, the grievous circum-

---

97.   Ibid., p. 453.
98.   Ibid., p.307.
99.   Ibid., pp. 356 - 7.
100. Ibid., p.373.

stances, and tell over our many flittings, our often relapsing, our wretched continuing in them; it would set our sorrow in passion, it would bring down some—some would come; our hearts would turn, our repentings roll together, and lament we would the death of our soul as we do otherwise lament the death of a friend, and for the unkindness we have showed to God as for the unkindness we do that man shows us.

But to repent adequately all takes time; it is not something done in the twinkling of an eye.

But this will ask time.... It is not a business of a few minutes; it will ask St. Peter's "retired place," and St. Paul's, "vacant time." It would ask a Nazarite's vow to do it as it should be done.... This I wish we would try. But we seek no place, we allow no time for it. Other affairs take up so much as can spare little or none for this, which the time will come when we shall think it the weightiest affair of all.[101]

However, if we do not repent of our sins we act contrary to God's will and pleasure. Although "our repentance and our unrighteousness hurts Him not," yet God is sorry for us as it is not his desire for us to be perpetually rebellious. Andrewes thus questioned whether we shall "continually 'fall' and never 'rise'?"[102]

Not to repent is also contrary "to the very light of nature" and to our "tutors" (the stork, turtle, crane, and swallow) which teach us "how to carry ourselves."[103] Will these "swallows fly over me and put me in mind of my 'return,' and shall not I heed them? Shall God still in vain hearken for *quid feci?* [what have I done?]" For Andrewes, the better response was, "I shall not see them fly but I shall think of the season of my returning."

"It has seemed good to the Holy Spirit" and to her to order there will be a solemn set return once in the year at least. And reason; for once a year all things turn.... The earth and all her plants, after a dead winter, return to the first and best season of the year.

---

101.   Ibid., p.369.
102.   Ibid., p. 354.
103.   Ibid., pp.340, 349.

The creatures, the fowls of the air, the swallow and the turtle, and the crane and the stork, "know their seasons," and make their just return at this time every year. Everything now turning that we also would make it our time to turn to God in.

However, if the swallow and other birds

serve not, as masters to teach us, they will serve as a quest to condemn us whom neither our own custom, reason, religion...nor...the light of nature, can bring to know so much as they.... This we should learn, but this we do not.[104]

Yet, if we observed them properly, Andrewes suggested that these birds might teach us good habits about repentance.
Firstly:

"They have a time." The place, the climate, which the cold of the weather makes them to leave, they fail not but find a time to turn back thither again. This they teach us first who in this respect less careful and more senseless than they, find a time and times many, often and long, to take our flight from God; occasioned by no cold or evil weather for commonly we do it when times are best and fairest; but we can find no time, not so much as half a time, to make our return in.

Secondly:

They have a certain time, when if you wait for them you shall be sure to see them come, and come at their appointed season; they will not miss. It will not be long, but you will see the swallow here again. This they teach us second; us who have sometimes some little persuasion *in modico*..."we can never find a convenient set time for it." Return we shall, that we will, but are still to seek for our season; and ever we will do, and never we do it.

Thirdly:

They have their certain time, and they know it. What time of the year the time of their return is, is commonly known; who knows not when swallows' time is? And our ignorance in not discerning

---

104.   Ibid., pp. 355, 357.

this point does God justly upbraid us withal; and bids us, if we know not what time to take, to get us to these fowls, and to take their time, the time they return at; that is, now, even this time, this season of the year; to return with the swallows, and to take our flight back when they do theirs. Rather do thus than waste our lives as we do, and take none at all. [105]

Many, however, fail to note the annual return of these birds and their message to us. Andrewes thus stressed that our "greatest errors in this matter of repentance came from our ignorance in not discerning of the time when we may have it, or our negligence in not using it when we discern it." We do not realise "that time is at this time now; now do these fowls return. Who knows whether he lives to see them return anymore? It may be the last spring, the last swallow-time, the last Wednesday of this name or nature, we shall ever live, to hear this point preached. Why do we not covenant then with ourselves not to let this time slip?" Everything points to this time; "The Church has fixed her season at it. And nature itself seems to favour it, that at the rising of the year we should rise, and return when the zodiac returns to the first sign."[106]

If we cannot learn repentance from nature and her creatures, stated Andrewes, perhaps we can learn judgment from them, which can also lead to repentance. There are two applications of this judgment. Firstly, it means "*judicium Domini,*" that is:

…that within us which is answerable to that secret instinct whereby the fowls are inclined to do this, which is the prick and *dictamen* of our conscience, the impression whereof is apparent in the most miscreant on earth; in whom nature itself shrinks and sighs when it has done amiss, and enjoys and lifts up itself when it has well done; and by which we are moved inwardly, as they by their instinct, to return, but that the motion with us passes, and with them not.

Secondly:

---

105. Ibid., pp. 350-1.
106. Ibid., p. 355.

Judicium Domini also conveyed His visitation hanging over our heads, called therefore judgment, because it comes not casually, but judicially proceeds from God; that is, when God calls to judgment by invasion, by scarcity, by gentle, general diseases, and such like; and then the complaint is, that where we should imitate these fowls and return against the sweet spring and fair time of the year, that is, while the days of peace and prosperity last, we are so far behind them, as not against fair, no not against foul, against neither we can be brought to it; not in the days of adversity—no not against the winter of our life.

However, unlike the fowls which "regard nature's inclination, so as every spring [is] sure to come; we have lost our regard so even of judgment and all, as neither vernal nor hibernal repentance we bring forth." Indeed, we seem to have no regard for "the everlasting judgment of the Lord...to which sooner or later we must all come, and there receive the sentence under execution whereof we shall lie eternally." Andrewes pleaded that we be more aware "that the time of returning is coming," and if we meditated upon it, it would "make us fly as fast back as any fowl of them all." [107]

Another image that Andrewes used to teach on repentance was a circle. "Repentance itself is nothing else but 'a kind of circling' to return to Him by repentance from Whom by sin we have turned away." This circle consists of two turnings:

> One is to be done with the "whole heart"...the other with it "broken and rent." First, a "turn," wherein we look forward to God, and with our "whole heart" resolve to "turn" to Him. Then a turn again wherein we look backward to our sins wherein we have turned from God, and with beholding them our very heart breaks.

These two turns are both crucial: the first involves "conversion from sin," resolving to amend our lives in the future; the second requires contrition for sin, reflecting on and being penitent for the past. In other words, "One declining from evil to be done hereafter; the other sentencing itself for evil done heretofore.... These two between them...[make] a perfect revolution."[108]

---

107. Ibid., pp.352-3.
108. Ibid., pp.358-9.

Andrewes believed that "the true turn is *ad Me*, so from sin as to God. 'To Me,' then, and 'with the heart;' And this is also needful." Yet for some this turning is "of the brain only," and does not involve "the heart," which is Joel's meaning. Yet true conversion "requireth not only alteration of the mind but of the will, a change not of certain notions only in the head, but of the affections of this heart too.... Nay, heart and all must turn. Not the face for shame, or the feet for fear; but the heart for very hatred of sin also."[109] So we spend all our lives navigating the circumference of this circle.

> When we commit sin, we die, we are dead in sin; when we repent, we revive again; when we repent ourselves of our repenting and relapse back, then sin rises again from the dead; and so *toties quoties*. And even upon these two, as two hinges, turns our whole life. All our life is spent in one of them.[110]

Andrewes also advocated that our repentance should have some "passion" to it, but mostly "we are so dead and dull when we are about it." However, it should not come "from 'dead works'... but have a life in it." This it will if the Holy Spirit guides us as He "still chooses to express it under some term of passion, as sorrow, fear, anger and the like, rather than the other way.... For passions be quick, there is life in them... He would have us affectionate when we are about this work, and not...cold and...calm."

Of all these passions "there is none quicker than that of anger." Anger rightfully should be for our sins, and for grieving God by them. Yet for the most part our anger is used "most where [it] should be least, and again least where [it] should be most. For take...a worldly man, and let him but overreach himself in some good bargain, in matter of profit, you will see him so angry, so out of patience with himself as often it casts him into some disease." There is indeed a "spirit" here from which we can learn, and apply it to our repentance.[111]

So Ash Wednesday is given to us to repent and "for an abstinence from sin," those sins which for "a trifle...certain carats of

---

109. Ibid., pp. 363-4.
110. Ibid., pp. 200 - 2.
111. Ibid., pp. 437 -8.

gain...a few minutes of delight" in which we indulge. It is also the day in which we reflect how our sins do offend "so presumptuously against so glorious a Majesty, [and]...so unkindly against...[a] loving...Saviour."[112] It is also the day when we ask God to help us poor sinners and to be merciful unto us. Yet on this penitential and fast day God's main complaint against us is not "that we fall and err, but that we rise not and return not; that is, still delay, still put off our repentance." If we act like this then we are acting contrary "to our own course and custom in other things" because if a man slips and falls he does not "lie still like a beast" but gets up immediately. Sin therefore must be understood as "a fall," which brings us down, "down from the state of Paradise, down to the dust of death, down to the bar of judgment, down to the pit of hell." Although we cannot escape being tainted with original sin at our birth, we can still flee from actual sin. "To become matchable with beasts, that is our fault, our great fault." Just as we rise from our bodily spills, so we must from our spiritual ones.[113]

It is not hard to imagine why Andrewes always addressed this urgency for repentance. Death comes often like the twinkling of an eye. Thus we must be prepared for it as unrepentant sin deadens our souls. "O the damp and mist of our sin! so great that it darkens not only the light of religion which God teaches, but even the light of nature which her instinct teaches, even the reasonless creature itself." And if we do nothing about it, if we do not repent, we "lose heaven...[and] must to hell." It simply was not possible "not to repent and not to perish." [114]

Indeed, Andrewes was rather impatient towards those who felt no need of repenting who "pass the whole course of...life, and, in the whole course of...life, not to be able to set down, where, or when, or what we did, when we did that which we call repenting; what fruits there came of it; what those fruits might be worth." It is only "a little before our death (and as little as may be), not till the world have given us over, then, lo, to come to our *quid faciemus?* to ask, *what should we do* ? when we are able to do nothing." Such an attitude towards repentance, Andrewes insisted, was not the New

---

112. Ibid.,, pp. 322, 367.
113. Ibid., pp.339, 342, 349.
114. Ibid., pp.349, 426,429.

Testament teaching. "This way, this fashion of repenting St. John knew it not; it is far from *fructus dignos*; St. Paul knew it not; it is far from his *opera digna*. And I can say little to it, but I pray God it deceive us not."[115]

For Andrewes to pass by the opportunity provided by Lent would be foolish. Although repentance is "good all year long," and never is "amiss"—indeed "it may be taken every day, for repentance would be as familiar to us as sin itself" —yet there are some times more apt to encourage repentance. Such is Lent! It may be "the last swallow time." Let us heed his warning!

---

115. Ibid., pp. 449 - 51.

CHAPTER SIX
THE PERENNIAL DISCIPLINE: FASTING

It is a custom this of the Church's while
it was a Christo recens, "yet fresh
and warm from Christ"; the Church
which was the Mother of the Apostles
themselves at all times kept, everywhere
observed, there and ever since.[116]

As Andrewes taught it, fasting was part of the disciplinary life of Christians, which was held "in high esteem...in frequent practice, of admirable performance...in the prime of Christianity" in practising Christ's example.

At Antioch, where "the disciples were first called Christians," we find them at their fast.... Our Saviour said to them, "When He was gone they should fast." So they did. St. Paul for one did it "oft." And for the rest they approved themselves for Christ's ministers..."by their fasting." And what themselves did, they advised others to do, even to "make them a vacant time to fast in."

He informed his contemporaries "which of the Fathers have not Homilies yet extant in the praise of it? What story of their lives but reports strange things of them in this kind?" To those who ignored the Church's teaching on fasting, Andrewes suggested, "either we must cancel all antiquity, or we must acknowledge the constant use and observation of it in the Church of Christ."[117]

---

116. Ibid., p. 392.

Of all the fasts observed in the primitive Church, Lent was kept as the great fast and has continued ever since in the Church, albeit in a milder form in the West as compared with the East. In the English Post-Reformation Church the Prayer Book had retained the old fasting days of Lent, Fridays, the vigils before major feasts and Ember days. Despite the Prayer Book rubric, fasting was neglected for the most part, except when a public fast was proclaimed or kept by the Puritans for some particular cause. Thus, having in mind how Puritans kept their fasts[118] rather than as commanded by the Church, Andrewes declared, "shall our fasting be altogether when we will ourselves? Shall it not also be some time when the Church will? May we bind ourselves, and may not she also bind us? Hath she no interest in us, no power over us?" The Puritans had seemed to have forgotten that just as "the Synagogue of the Jews...had power to prescribe fasts and did," so has "our Mother, the Church of Christ." In case they thought fasting only a late invention brought in by "Popery," he informed them that "the Council of Gangra[119] hath laid an anathema on them that keep it not." To counter the argument that to fast is being "like Papists," he declared how disillusioned such men are, as if "not to fast is made a *supersedeas* to all Popery, as if that alone were enough to make us truly Reformed." They should know that the precepts of fasting, and its twin, repentance, "were made in the times under the persecution, the very best times of the Church, [and] lay forth plainly what is to be followed and observed in this kind." So strongly did Andrewes feel about this disregard of the Church's teaching on fasting that at the beginning of his sermon on Ash Wednesday for 1622/

---

117. Ibid., pp. 379-80

118. Puritans, when they organised a fast day, took a day off work in order to devote the whole day (8 a.m. to 3 p.m.) to some religious exercise and as a means of almsgiving. For example, in the Dedham classis their almsgiving went to the poor and the "ffrench church." This classis also expressed a concern that many of its poor could not keep a fast as they simply could not afford to miss a day's wages. R.G. Ussher, *Presbyterian Movement in the Reign of Queen Elizabeth as illustrated by the Minute Book of the Dedham Classis 1582 - 1589*, Camden Society, 3rd Series, Vol. 8 (London, 1905). pp. 29, 66, 68.

119. Held in c.341 it passed twenty canons directed against a false asceticism. Canon twenty-one explained the true nature of asceticism.

1623 he reiterated his plea for a deliverance from Puritan "malicious slander" on fasting. Thus he declared that he would rather "spend the hour in speaking again for the duty to have it done, than to deal with the caution what to eschew in the doing." If "we cannot get men to it, to fast; what need we then spend any speech how they should not do it, when they do it not?"[120]

To other contemporaries, who for "the most part seem so faintly persuaded of fasting as if it were no needful part of a Christian man's duty," Andrewes declared that not only was it Christ's method for the mortification of the body, but his speaking of it in the present tense "when ye fast," in the same way as he told us to pray, meant he wanted us to fast. "Christ cannot say, 'When ye fast,' if we fast not at all." Consequently, if we do not "turn to [God] with fasting" we must be ready "to show a good cause why, and to show it to God." That we are meant to fast is also reflected in the Church's appointed readings for Ash Wednesday, otherwise another epistle and Gospel would have been appointed. Andrewes also indicated that other professionals such as physicians, philosophers, and politicians advocated fasting for different reasons and motives. However, the gains from fasting for "religious motives" are far more worthy and more numerous than those gained for medical, philosophical, or political reasons.[121]

Furthermore, Andrewes argued that if men practised fasting when faced with many natural circumstances (such as disaster, grief, and anger), "why not for the grief of our grievous offences? for fear of being drowned in perdition eternal. Why not for indignation of our many indignities offered to God?" If we fast for our sins it "shows our affections of sorrow, anger, fear, desire, are quick, have life, are very affections indeed in secular matters; but dead and dull, and indeed no affections at all but plain counterfeits in things pertaining to God, or that concern the estate and hazard of our souls."[122]

Those who refused to fast, he believed, were no different from those of antiquity who also questioned fasting. For instance, in the Old Testament Zechariah indicated that many shrugged "at their

---

120. Andrewes, Vol. 1, pp. 391-2, 398-9, 403.
121. Ibid., pp. 367, 375-6, 378.
122. Ibid., pp. 386-7.

fasts" and grumbled "What, and must we fast still? Yet more fasting? Have we not fasted enough, and have done it thus and thus long?" However, they could not escape from it, for "the Prophet held them to it and would not release them." Neither was it any different in the New Testament. In describing the New Covenant's practice, Andrewes declared:

> I had rather you heard St. Augustine than myself; *Ego*, saith he, *animo revolvens*, &c. "I going over in my mind the writings of the Evangelists and Apostles in the New Testament, see fasting is commanded, there is a precept for fasting." So fasting is in precept there if we will trust St. Augustine's eyes. And we may. He that in this place saith, *cum jejunatis*, "when ye fast," saith in another, *tum jejunabunt*, "then they shall fast" and that amounts to a precept, I trow.

Since then "the Church for this day" has given "us an Epistle out of the Old Testament and a Gospel out of the New...she did it for this end, to show that fasting has the wings of both Cherubin to cover it; both Testaments, Old and New; Joel for the one, Christ for the other."[123]

What then did fasting actually mean for Andrewes? It meant exactly what it always meant: having one meal each day and forgoing "dainty alluring meat." This was the type of fasting practiced by David, who fasted until the sun went down. However, if that fasting was too hard, Andrewes suggested that "the Church as an indulgent mother, mitigates all she may; enjoins not for fast that of David," but also accepts the fast of Daniel which is "to forbear *cibos desiderii*, and 'flesh.'" If his contemporaries rejected these two kinds of fast, Andrewes insisted "a third I find not"; there is simply no other kind of fast ever practised by Christians. However, by the grace of God all should be able to fast according to Daniel's method, as that was really practising abstinence, which is "'to deny ourselves that we might, for doing that we might not.'" Of course, what applied to food also applied to drink. Fasting acts therefore as "a chastisement for sin" and also as "a medicinal force, a special good remedy to prevent sin." He stressed that "if by abstinence we crop

---

123.   Ibid., pp. 378 -80.

not the buds of sensuality, they will ripen and seed to the ruin of our souls."[124]

Andrewes also made it clear that when we are serious about our fasting as an act of devotion to our Lord, the devil will do his utmost to persuade us not to fast at all, offering "us a license not to keep Lent, to keep what diet we will." Thus "when we have... resolved that fast we will, and when we will, and we set ourselves seriously to it," are we safe? "Will the devil be gone away?... No indeed; but hovers about us still, as if there were yet somewhat for him to do." Just as he tempted our blessed Saviour, "when the 'Spirit led Him into the wilderness,' and He fell to His fast," so we must expect the devil to tempt us in like manner. We are never out of his reach by eating or fasting, as he "attends our feasts, 'to make our table a snare;' attends our fasts, 'to turn them' as well as our prayers 'into sin.' Eating, he is busy with us to make us eat like Esau. Fasting, no less busy to make us fast like the Pharisee." Satan also tricks us with the notion of hypocrisy, persuading us not to fast and to make suspect "some sparks of a Pharisee" in those who preach on fasting. If Satan cannot use hypocrisy as a reason for not fasting, he has a third temptation: suggesting we do it for our own glory and vanity, rather than for God and our own humility. This is what Andrewes called a "stage fast," where by looks one appears to fast, but inwardly there is no thought of contrition, humility, and honesty.[125]

To those who succumb to this temptation and make fasting their "reward, to be seen of men," do have their reward now, but in so doing they forsake the eternal reward which is Heaven. Yet it really is not a "reward" but a "punishment," for although it would seem there is "no great harm to receive a reward of praise," yet when "man's praise" is weighed against God's, it is but a poor thing and of no eternal value. The end result of all these temptations is to "keep no Lent, not to fast at all." However, God's way is to use fasting as "one of the nails of the cross to which the flesh is fastened" and as a help against temptation, as illustrated by Christ himself, who fasted in the wilderness "before His temptation." After all, the end result of fasting is that we "fast to God, not to the world; to our

---

124.   Ibid., pp.368, 388-9.
125.   Ibid., pp. 401, 407-8.

hearts, not to other men's eyes; to conscience, not to form; not to set us up a stage to do it, but with Christ to do it apart 'in secret.'"[126]

Andrewes also coupled fasting with the virtue of temperance. He described "a man that cannot refraine his appetite" to be "like a City broken downe and without walls." From his own practice, he stated that our daily allowance should "be just as much, and no more, than will serve to hold life and soul together." Eating "a smaller repast" means there is always some to give to the poor—a continual plea by Andrewes. Although "meat is for the belly and we be debtors to the flesh...we must never live after the flesh; she must not be accustomed to have what she call for," otherwise it will never be tamed by temperance. Thus temperance was another way of disciplining the body, which should never dominate and over-shadow the soul. "It keeps us from the graves of lust...it preserves reason which is the power of the minde," and it "will make men depart from the flesh and grow spiritually, and so be like the divine nature." Patience is tied to temperance; Andrewes asked, "What makes a man intemperate but impatience?" Therefore patience is another virtue the faithful need to acquire in order to live an ascetic life.[127]

By joining our fasting with repentance, together with our pray-ing and almsgiving, we can be assured that Lent will give us the preparation needed to welcome Christ as our risen Saviour at the great Easter Vigil.

---

126. Ibid., pp. 381, 389, 400-2, 407, 416.
127. Ibid., Vol. 6, p. 236; *Apos. Sacra* p.634.

CHAPTER SEVEN
THE PERENNIAL GIVING:
ALMSGIVING AND CHARITY

Charity is a duty to be extended to all,
both Jews and Gentiles, as well as to
Christians.[128]

Andrewes thought of almsgiving in mediæval terms, "a work of mercy" because it is so acceptable unto God that he pours his mercy upon the almsgiver. He also expressed it as "a work of charity" when we share "our goods" with others, and, more specifically, when we share them with the poor, for "in the tidings of the Gospel they are not left out." One of the characteristics of the Liturgy when celebrated by Andrewes was that communicants were asked to give a separate almsgiving for the poor when returning to their seats after receiving the Sacrament.

So it is not surprising that Andrewes pleaded with the rich of London to help the destitute and hungry during the frequent famines of his age. He maintained that in actual fact it took little of a man's wealth to keep the poor. Accordingly, in his Lenten sermon in 1593/4 he preached, "[T]hat our goods may go, not to some end, nor to some good end, but the very best end of all, the relief of the poor." He stated that he would have applauded Judas' outcry against the extravagance of Mary Magdalene towards Christ, if it had been for the right reason. Of course, there should be nourishment for "many hundreds" rather than ointment for one, "necessary relief"

---

128. Ibid., p. 635.

rather than "needless delight"; "continual good" rather than "a transistory smell"; "many hungry bellies filled" rather than "one head anointed."[129]

In his lecture on Genesis 4:9 he made clear that God "will call us to account, not only for the breach of faith towards himself...but for breach of charity one man towards another."[130] To illustrate the depth and breadth of Christian charity, Andrewes took St. Paul's application of it to the Corinthians in both his 1596 Lenten sermon at Court and in his sermon shortly afterwards at St. Giles. He indicated how Paul's charity was consistently lavished on them, even though it was never returned. This is love without hope, as Bernard called it, or love in its highest form, in that it is prepared "to spend and be spent...and be spent most willingly." Paul's attitude manifested for Andrewes the essential difference between Christian and pagan charity. The former "shew[s], not only *brotherly love* to Christians, but *charity* to all men." Christian charity is "pliant...ever ready to transform itself to whatsoever may have likelihood to prevail".[131]

In his own day Andrewes accused many of his contemporaries of not following Paul's example and thereby failing to fulfill the second great commandment "to love thy neighbor." In the words of James, quoted by Andrewes, "if thy brother starve, and thou sayest depart and be warm, but minister not to him," what charity is that?[132] One of the reasons Andrewes maintained for showing charity to those outside of the Church was that "they be wonne" for the Church. To do this is to imitate the love of God in his son who sought all outcasts.

It was in his Spital Sermon in Easter Week of 1588, one of his very early sermons, that he first addressed the need for charity by all, even the poor, but especially the affluent, who often acted like Dives. He told them to "lift up your eyes and see the streets round about you, 'the harvest is verily great and the labourers few.'" Now "hear your charge. I pray you." He reminded them that they "have the substance...to 'do good.'" Therefore "Be rich in good works"

---

129. Andrewes, Vol. 1, pp. 443-5, Vol. 2, p.42.
130. *Apos Sacra.*, pp. 415.
131. Ibid., p. 639; Andrewes, Vol. 2, pp. 101-2.
132. *Apos. Sacra*, p. 638.

rather than "good words," as Paul taught, and then they will be "rich indeed." Andrewes warned them—and us too:

> There is no avoiding, you must needs seal this fruit of well-doing, you must needs do it. For having wealth and wherewithal to "do good," if you do it not, *imprimis*, talk not of faith, for you have no faith in you; if you have wherewith to shew it and shew it not.

Furthermore, "if you do it not...now" as I have warned you, on that "great day" you will be judged "not of your trust and confidence, or any other virtues, though they be excellent, but of your feeding, clothing, visiting, harbouring, succouring, and in a word, of your well-doing only." [133]

To convince them of their duty to give alms, he implored them to ponder on the story of Dives and Lazarus in the gospel of St. Luke. Andrewes implied that our Lord told this parable to unlock "hell-gates to let us see it." The teaching from that is clear: "There shall be never a rich man with Lazarus in his bosom in heaven, unless he have had a Lazarus in his bosom here on earth." Therefore "remember Lazarus...you may find Lazarus if you seek him, everyday."[134] Thus they must spread their mantle over the poor. Andrewes suggested there were two kinds of poor his contemporaries could help:

> [One sort] shall be with us "always," as Christ saith, to whom we must do good by relieving them: such is the comfortless estate of poor captives, the succourless estate of poor orphans, the desolate estate of the poor widows, the distressed estate of poor strangers, the discontented estate of poor scholars; all of which must be suffered and succoured too.

> There are others...beggars and vagabonds able to work; to whom good must be done, by not suffering them to be as they are, but to employ them in such sort as they may do good.

He further challenged the affluent who were "rich in coffer" to be "rich in conscience," as this you will "carry with you, your coffers

---

133. Andrewes, Vol. 5. 35-38.
134. Ibid., Vol. 2, pp. 79, 96.

you shall not." So it is "in God's book," not in bankbooks, that eternal life lies.

> The true riches are the riches of "His glorious inheritance." They
> be the true riches, which except a man can assure himself of after
> the lease of his life is out, he shall be in a marvellous poor case, as
> was the rich man; and beg of Lazarus there, that begged of him
> here. Those riches must be thought of, marry then you must be
> "rich in good works." Not to give something to somebody at some
> time. Why? who doth not so? That is not to be "rich."

By this Andrewes meant if we only "give sparingly, a piece of bread or a draught of drink...to the brother of low estate" this is not almsgiving; it is not a work of mercy at all as it has cost nothing.[135]

Andrewes also reminded his affluent contemporaries that God had placed the poor on this earth to enable the rich to share their wealth with them. After all, all "bounty" came from him, and all that we have is not "ours" but "His." Therefore "'that God Which gave asketh but His own.'" Moreover, it may be that one day we may be destitute. Applying the parable of the sower, he proclaimed:

> The seed is your alms, the ground is the poor, you are the sowers.
> When it is therefore sown among them, how it is spent, or what
> becomes of it, you know not; yet this you know, and may reckon,
> that at the fulness of time, at the harvest of the end of the world,
> for every grain of temporal contribution, you shall receive an ear
> of eternal retribution. Whereas, storing it up here, it may after
> your decease be stored for harlots and gamesters and rioters, in
> whose hands it shall corrupt and putrify, and yourselves lose the
> fruit thereof for ever. By this comparison you may know, that
> when you are dealing for the poor, it is your own business you
> intend; that not forgetting them, you remember yourselves; pity-
> ing them, you have pity on your own souls, and that "your labour
> shall not be in vain in the Lord."[136]

In his own prayers Andrewes manifested all too clearly that the "poor" are not just the "hungry, thirsty, naked," but also "prisoner, strangers, harbourless, [and the] unburied." It also includes "orphans"

---

135. Ibid., Vol. 5, pp. 43 - 4.
136. Ibid., pp. 44, 47.

and "widows," those "condemned to die," the sick in soul [and] body" and those "possessed by the Devil." All of these must be visited and cared for as our brothers and sisters in Christ, "from the heart." This is our "greatest business, we make it not our least care."[137]

It is also clear that when Andrewes taught about acts of charity, he also included a spiritual component. Thus charity meant forgiving those who injure us in any way and praying for our neighbor and his needs, thus doing what James directed—to pray for one another. Indeed, as James also said, "Charity covers a multitude of sin."[138] In the next chapter, Andrewes' teaching on the Lord's Prayer clearly defined the boundaries of our charity.

137.   Ibid., Vol. 2, p. 96, Vol. 11, p. 263.
138.   H. Issacson, *Institutiones Piae* (London, 1630), p. 12.

CHAPTER EIGHT
PERENNIAL COMMUNICATION:
PRAYING

Of all the parts of God's service,
prayer justly challengeth the
first place.[139]

Above all else Andrewes was a praying man, and he wanted his contemporaries to be so too. For Andrewes there is never a time when we do not "stand in need of God's particular assistance," nor find ourselves in a place where we cannot pray. What he was advocating was that prayer should be ceaseless; it was like the burning of incense ever arising to the court of Heaven. "'Let our prayer go up to Him that His grace may come down to us,' so to lighten us in our ways and works that we may in the end come to dwell with Him, in the light 'whereof there is no even-tide.'"[140]

It is through prayer that we come to know God better and learn that it is only by the Holy Spirit working within us that we can pray at all. Prayer is thus a gift of grace. So, if we find ourselves not being able to pray, we must humbly ask for grace to be able to pray. Without praying we sin, and so one of Andrewes' terse remarks was that "prayer is good as it keeps us from sin."

For many, their introduction to Lancelot Andrewes has been through his *Preces Privatæ*. Those familiar with this collection will know that his prayers are like a piece of tapestry woven of strands

---

139.   Ibid., p. 1.
140.   Andrewes. Vol. 3. p. 376.

from the Bible, especially the Psalms, the Offices, the Prayer Book he loved, and those prayers that have echoed down the centuries. However, this weaving was not tight, but was loose enough to allow for spontaneous prayer arising out of daily life.

His own prayer pattern followed the Church's daily offices with its five-fold approach—confession, thanksgiving, praise, intercession, and petition for morning and evening prayers. All of these were extensive. For instance, in confession he repeatedly saw himself as the "chief of sinners" and thus showed "the infinite acknowledgement of unworthiness and want, and the infinite hope in God's mercy and love, in one who searched and judged himself with keen and unflinching truth."[141]

Prayer for Andrewes was also ecclesial and sacramental, and thus the *Preces* cannot be separated from Andrewes' theology. It revealed his consciousness of continuing in the line of the Fathers, or indeed further back to antiquity when man first set up his altar to God, and therefore there was always an awareness of praying as part of that whole Church of God—the saints and sinners, the living and the dead. This is evident by what can be termed an *anamnesis* approach to his praying, where he constantly recalled the various gifts God has given through creation, redemption, and sanctification. He also firmly believed that Christ and the Church's teaching spoke as "one person," and that outside of the Church no Christian could receive Christ's blessings and grace, which in time will bring them to "the glory, the joys, [and] the crown of Heaven."[142]

Andrewes' prayers embraced the whole cosmos, ranging from nature—with all its wondrous details—to the needs of those around him. Everything must be offered to God, either in praise and thanksgiving for the whole universe or as a confession of penitence for soiling it. He prayed "for all commonwealths of the world" and for all peoples, whether they worked in mines or courts. More particularly, his prayers included all those who had been associated with him in any way during his life. So he prayed for his old school and master, college, parishes, and cathedrals. Furthermore, his bidding prayers supported his ecclesial teaching. In the fragility of the

---

141.   R. W. Church, *Paschal and other Sermons* (London, 1895), p. 7;
         Andrewes. Vol. 11, pp. 244, 246, 253, 276.
142.   Ibid., 1, pp. 15, 373, Vol. 2, p. 367.

"whole Militant Church, scattred farre and wide over the face of the whole earth," he prayed for the preserving of "those trueths that it hath recovered from the sundrie grose and superstitious errors of the former age." He also prayed for its unity, which it daily seems to lose "through the unchristian and unhappy contentions of these dayes of ours."

> For the Catholic Church:
> for the churches throughout the world:
> their truth, unity and stability to wit:
> in all let charity thrive, truth live:
> for our own church:
> that the things that are wanting therein be supplied,
> that are not right be set in order.[143]

In praying for the whole church Andrewes never forgot that the Church militant was part of the wider Church and its saints— especially the Mother of God and all heavenly beings. Accordingly, in an intercessory prayer for the whole Church collated from the liturgies of James and Chrysostom, he concluded with:

> Neither are we unmindful to bless Thee, for the most holy, pure, highly blessed, the Mother of God, Mary the eternal Virgin, with all the Saints:
> Recommending ourselves and our whole life to Thee,
> O Lord, our Christ and God:
> For to Thee belongeth glory, honour, and worship.[144]

Overall, his prayers ranged from his own sense of utter unworthiness and frailty to the grandeur and wonder of God, and from the humble needs of the individual to the demanding needs of the State. There seemed to be nothing that escaped his prayerfulness, even for those who had committed suicide. So his prayers reflected his concern for all humanity, as they embraced king and subject, rich and poor, and each man in his various daily work and circum-

---

143. Ibid., Vol. 11, pp. 260 - 1, 263-4, 270-2, 278, 286-7, 294, 296, 310, 313-4; F. E. Brightman, (Ed & Trans), *The Private Devotions of Lancelot Andrewes*, (Gloucester, Mass, 1978), p.32.

144. Andrews, Vol. 11, p. 295.

stance; for all creation, for the entire world, and, of course, for the universal church, "Let us beg of the Lord for the whole creatures, the gift of Healthful, Fruitful, Peaceful times."[145]

However, the *Preces Privatæ* is not the only extant work of Andrewes' prayers and his teaching on prayer. Shortly after his death in 1630, his amanuensis and chaplain, Henry Isaacson, compiled from Andrewes' papers a collection of prayers to cover every aspect of life. As well as prayers for the morning and evening, there were also prayers for the Eucharist, in sickness and approaching death. Titled *Institutiones Piæ*, or *Directions to Prayer*, it also included the seven penitential and thanksgiving psalms, and summaries of Andrewes' teaching on the Lord's Prayer, the Ten Commandments, repentance, and confession.

There is yet another important work on prayer by Andrewes: *Scala Coeli*, first published in 1611, is a collection of 19 sermons that he gave on prayer and the Lord's Prayer, probably in the 1590's; its title is not without significance. In the Mediæval Church, "Scala Coeli" was intricately bound up with indulgences meant to lessen the time of purgatory through prayers, masses, penances, and good works offered for the dead. At the beginning of the Henrician Reformation, it was one of the abuses that clearly needed to be put away. It had also been one of the pilgrimage cults of Westminster Abbey when, in 1500, "Henry VII secured the 'Scala Coeli' indulgence for requiem Masses celebrated in his new chapel."[146]

On the title page, the editor, Francis Burton, depicted the purpose of these sermons, "the first sixe guiding to the true Doore," and the rest "teaching how so to knock thereat that wee may enter."[147] Hence prayer must always be the way to Heaven, though offered simply in gratitude for what God has given, without the implication of any leniency on Judgment Day.

Here is a brief summary of these sermons. In the first of the preparatory ones Andrewes emphasised the importance of preparation in order to be able to pray aright. The first step is to acknowl-

145.   Ibid., pp. 260-1, 253, 271-2, 296.

146.   E. Duffy, *The Stripping of the Altars, Traditional Religion in England 1440 - 1580*, (Yale , 1993). pp. 375 - 6.

147.   L. Andrewes, *Scala Coeli: Nineteene Sermons Concerning Prayer* (London, 1611), *Dedicatory, A4.*

edge our own lack of holiness, goodness, and sufficiency without God. That acknowledgement leads to the door of prayer, and, on opening it, we will firstly confess our unworthiness and need for spiritual enlightenment, strength, and humility. Only then will God give his grace to meet our needs.[148] In his own prayer book, Andrewes had a meditation before prayer.[149]

The second sermon was directed particularly towards those who thought they could pray in their own strength. They forget that "every good giving and every perfect gift cometh" from God, including the gift (what "St. Paul calls grace") to be able to pray. From grace there is a "spiritual" enlightenment and gradual progression "from one degree of perfection to another" for the rest of our earthly life. Thus it is only by grace that we can perfect the imperfect. This is what Andrewes often called "growing in holiness" in other sermons.[150]

The emphasis of the third sermon is on our obedience in praying according to Christ's precepts, and, therefore, "we may not think any longer it is a matter indifferent." This meant praying publicly in a set form, the kind of prayer that has been offered since antiquity, and as such is like incense rising to the heavenly court.[151] Therefore, praying is not something we choose to do, but rather what we are bound to perform as being "required as part of God's service" and "worship." For Andrewes, partaking in the Divine Liturgy with the whole Church is the great act of praying; far more important than our own private prayers, yet he did not belittle private praying, as seen in this advice: [152]

---

148.   Andrewes, Vol. 5, pp. 301 - 310.

149.   Brightman, op. cit, p. 7.

150.   Andrewes, Vol. 5, pp. 311, 315.

151.   He explained why it was appropriate to speak of prayers rising like incense. "And it is most fitly resembled to incense, for the use of incense was to sweeten those places which are unsavoury; even so the wicked imaginations and unchaste thoughts of our hearts, which yield a stinking smell in the nostrils of God, are sweetened by no other means than by prayer; and therefore to shew how the one is resembles by the other, it is said that while the incense was burning, the people were without upon their knees in prayer." Ibid., p. 324. He also mades similar references in his Genesis lectures. *Apos Sacra*, pp. 125, 663.

152.   Andrewes, Vol. 5, pp. 321, 323.

When thou awakest in the morning, shut and close up the entrance to thy heart, from all unclean, profane, and evil thoughts, and let the consideration of God and goodness enter in.

When thou art arisen and art ready, return thyself to thy closet, or other private place, and offer to God, the first fruits of the day, and in praying to him and praising him, remember,

1. To give him thanks, for thy quiet rest received, for delivering thee from all dangers, ghostly and bodily, and for all other his benefits to thee.

2. Offer unto him thyself, and all things that thou dost possess, and desire him to dispose of thee and them, according to his good pleasure.

3. Crave his grace to guide thee, and to strengthen thee from, and against all temptations, that so thou mayest do nothing the day following contrary to his will.

4. And lastly, beg of him, (according to how we should pray) all things needful for the soul and body.[153]

Praying alone, to Andrewes, also meant those "private meditations and conferences between God and our souls": the contemplative approach. His liturgical sermons also often advocated this approach. For instance, in his extant sermons for Good Friday he begged his auditors to spend much time simply contemplating the cross. "Blessed are the hours that are so spent!" he told them.[154]

Sermon three details how private praying is closely linked with Christ's command to "ask, seek, knock." Obeying this command helps us, firstly, to "see our want and need" so that we shall ask for them; secondly, it enables us to acknowledge that "we have lost ourselves," and so we seek; thirdly, it enables us to learn that without God's grace we are shut out of his presence and kingdom until we knock. Andrewes again stressed our asking for the "spirit of grace and of prayer and…then shall we have ability and power not only to seek the door, but when we have found it to knock at it." Why does Andrewes put so much emphasis on the door? The reason is that Christians have to learn "that when we come to pray to God the whole person must be occupied," that is, "the lifting up of

---

153. *Inst. Piæ*, pp. 84 – 5.
154. Andrewes, Vol. 2, pp. 160, 163.

our eyes...hands...[and] heart." Only then will the door open through which we shall "enter into His kingdom."[155]

Employing the right kind of knocking led Andrewes to teach on the correct posture for prayer; he followed the example Christ gave. This method requires kneeling reverently—not sitting. He argued that we cannot ask for grace if we ourselves are "wanting unto grace."[156]

Andrewes, in his fourth sermon, stressed his ecclesial teaching. When we pray we are part of that whole church which prays unceasingly all over the world; however dispersed, the faithful always pray as "members of one body." These prayers are joined with those of "God's saints that pray for us with all instancy." Hence, the main emphasis in prayer is not praying privately for ourselves but corporately, so that when our praying is "faint" we are comforted by knowing that we not only have the saints and other Christians praying with us, but also "our Head, Christ...[who] ceaseth not to make request to God still for us." Of course it is he who prays in us and enables us to overcome our faintness and infirmities, so that our prayers will proceed from the "fervency and zeal" of the spirit. By acknowledging that it is "the Spirit of God [which] maketh intercession for us," we shall not err "in spiritual things" as he "will make that prayer for us which shall be both for our good and also according to God's will." Furthermore, praying as a member of the Church also teaches us that all Christians, living and departed, are bound together through the Holy Spirit.[157]

In the fifth sermon Andrewes suggested that we approach prayer through the eyes of the disciples, who learnt about prayer from observing Christ. From him they learnt three uses of prayer. One is "of necessity; for God hath left prayer to be our city of refuge, to the end that when all means fail we should fly unto God by prayer." The second is "of duty, for prayer is an offering," and in that sense is likened to incense, while the third is "of dignity," when prayer becomes a matter of being completely absorbed in God Himself. Thus, like the disciples, we can also learn to approach our Lord to "teach us to pray," and his response will be the same, "the

---

155. Ibid., Vol. 5, pp. 322, 324 - 5, 327.
156. Ibid., pp. 329.
157. Ibid. pp. 337, 339-40.

Lord's Prayer." This is the model for all our praying, in which "there is not one word wanting that should be put in, nor any word more than ought to be."[158]

In the last of these preparatory sermons Andrewes emphasised once again the ecclesial aspect of prayer in Christ's Church, as well as reiterating the themes of the previous five. One of Andrewes' prominent themes was "obedience" to God; that is, we pray according to God's precepts, which in turn meant that "service and duty which we owe to Him." Such precepts directed that we pray at "certain hours"; for lay-people that meant "three times a day" and for the clergy "seven times a day," as set down in Psalms 55:17 and 119:164. The place where we are to pray is in God's "dominion," and so the first requirement for prayer is that it be public, where priest and people gather to worship God in "the Liturgy and the public service of God." In public prayer Andrewes emphasised the importance of the office of the priest, the mediator between God and his people, who intercedes on behalf of them.

The Lord's Prayer, ever said by the Church, must be the framework of prayer, declared Andrewes. There are four parts, which are summarized under the two headings "of confession and petition." Under confession there is both *confessionem fraudis*—that is, "confession of sins"—and *"confessio laudis*, that is, thanksgiving to God for His goodness in pardoning our sins, and bestowing His benefits upon us." With petition there is both "comprecation and deprecation." The former seeks for good things, while the latter desires "that evil be removed." Included in our petitions is the prayer "proceeding from charity," which leads the Church to pray for all sorts and conditions of men, from those in authority to those with special needs, such as the sick and poor.[159]

At the end of this last preparatory prayer sermon, Andrewes commented that "we have need to be instructed in the sense of the Lord's Prayer," that prayer "penned by our Saviour Christ on behalf of His disciples and His Church unto the end of the world." In accordance with this, he gave sermons on each petition. Of all the prayers offered to God each day, he described the *Pater Noster* as the prayer of charity and fraternity because there is no "I," "mine,"

---

158.   Ibid., 344 - 5, 349.
159.   Ibid., 354, 356 - 60.

or "my," but rather "our" and "us." It is "our Father," "our bread," "our trespasses," and deliver "us" from evil. [160]

Our Father

When we pray "our Father," it should remind us that we are but one of God's children. He is the Father of us all, and consequently it should be "a pledge of our love" towards our brethren—what we pray for ourselves, we pray for others. Hence we pray that our brethren will be delivered from evil as well as ourselves; we pray that they with us will receive daily bread; and we pray that they and we, all sinners, need God's forgiveness. Moreover, we must also pray for those brethren who are our enemies, that God may have mercy upon them as well as ourselves.

The image of God as *Father* conveys all that fatherhood implies. His paternity covers all creation, but especially man. He provides for us; he never stops loving us; he wants to give us good things, but he will also chasten us when we need it. We, as his children, may forget our duty to our heavenly Father, but he never ceases to love us. He is always waiting for us to say "I will return to my Father." *Father* also reminds us that God made man in "His own image [and]...breathed into him life immortal," and after the fall rescued him by giving him "a second birth" to make him "the son of God" with an entrance "into the kingdom of God." Finally, *Father* assures us of the life to come with him in Heaven. [161]

Who art in Heaven

We are reminded that our Father dwells in Heaven on his throne in all his glory. This should in turn inspire us to pray with devotion and reverence to him who always provides our bodily and spiritual needs. As Tertullian said, "no Father so fatherly." It also conveys that, as God's children, Heaven is our native land, and we are but sojourners and pilgrims on this earth. As citizens of this higher realm, we must constantly lift up our hearts to Heaven so that we can have the image of God imprinted on our being, in order to seek the things above. In the life to come we have a lively hope, distinct from the dead hope of this life.[162]

---

160. Ibid., p. 361.
161. Ibid., pp. 361 - 2, 364, 366, 368-9.
162. Ibid., pp. 372 – 380, esp. p.375.

Hallowed be Thy Name

This is the first of the seven petitions, and it is the only one concerned with God. Hence, before seeking our own and our brethren's needs, we pray that God's name will be sanctified, as he alone is holy. As we ponder on the holiness of God, other manifestations of holiness should come to us, such as his day, the Church, his priests, the sacraments, creation, and our fellow brothers and sisters.

When we hallow his name we give God great delight and pleasure, and we join the angels in their *sanctus, sanctus, sanctus*. This petition also reminds us that we must not curse the Holy name, and that we must pray for those who do. We must also not give any glory to ourselves but only to God, as everything we have comes from him. When we reverence God's name it also helps us to fight the sin of pride, which is so rooted in us. Above all, the petition tells us of our true vocation:

> If while we remain on earth our whole desire be to sanctify God's name, we shall at length come to the place where we shall say and might sing as the Cherubims do, and with the heavenly host of Angels sing, "Glory to God on high"; we shall fall down before His throne, saying always, "Thou art worthy, O Lord, to receive glory, and honour and praise for ever."[163]

Thy kingdom come

This is the first of the six petitions that concern us. In the first three we petition for good things, whilst in the other three we pray "for the removing of evil." This petition speaks of the kingdom itself, and the coming of the kingdom. We may wonder how we can pray for the coming of God's kingdom when it already exists. Andrewes therefore made the distinction between the universal kingdom of God and the kingdom of glory for which Christ has taught us to pray, and which has been committed to him by the Father. It is this kingdom that still has its enemies: Satan, sin, and death, and it is only when all are conquered that the kingdom of glory will reign.

---

163.   Ibid., pp. 384, 389.

There is also the spiritual kingdom, called the kingdom of grace, which dwells within us. If we do not possess this kingdom we can never partake of the other kingdom, and therefore we must entreat the Holy Spirit to plant in our hearts all that is good and to drive out all that is evil, so that Satan and sin do not set up "their thrones in our hearts." Then we can be like the saints of old in their pursuit of the kingdom of glory, summed up in their prayer, "Maranatha."[164]

Thy will be done

Of course, to "obtain the kingdom of glory" God's will must be done. Not everyone who says, "Lord, Lord shall enter the kingdom of God, but he that shall do the will of my Father which is in heaven." Thus the door to the Kingdom opens by the doing of God's will. However, Andrewes declared that in essence it is "not so much that God's will may be done, but rather that what God willeth may be our will." We must not wrestle nor struggle against it, but patiently submit our wills to his, just as Christ manifested in the garden of Gethsemane. To be obedient to God's will two things are required:

1. To lay aside our own will and say "convert my froward and unwilling will into Thy will." If we find that our will is contrary to God's, then we must "pull it up by the roots."
2. To have "a baser conceit of our own will and a high and reverend opinion of God's." We must not trust "our reason and understanding" to direct our wills as this is "perverse," but only to God's grace to direct it.

Then we can be assured in our consciences that we have done the will of God, and we shall enjoy that "peace and joy of the Holy Spirit," "a pledge" to us "of the Kingdom of glory."[165]

In earth as it is in Heaven

In this petition we pray "that God's name may be sanctified in earth as it is in Heaven, for the accomplishment of his will on earth, and then for the consummation of his kingdom." The petition is also a reminder to keep our flesh in subjection so that the old Adam

---

164. Ibid., p.394.
165. Ibid., pp.396-7, 401, 404.

in us continues to make way to the new in Christ as commenced in our baptism.

We should also desire, while we live here on earth, that our conversation will be heavenly. Just as the angels and saints in Heaven fulfill God's commandments, we also pray that we may cheerfully labor like them, and that our carnal hearts may be applied to the meditation of Heaven to make us "saints in earth."

It reminds us too that Christ is both of Heaven and earth. As "the head of His Church" he is in Heaven, but in respect of his body, which is called Christ, he is on earth. Therefore, we also pray that the Church may do God's will, even as Christ the head does in Heaven.[166]

Give us this day our daily bread

In a sense this is all nature's prayer, for all creatures on earth and in the air call upon God for their sustenance. Yet there is a difference between them and us; they require only corporal food, but we also need spiritual food, which is the heavenly manna received at the Eucharist.

We ask for "bread" because without it we cannot serve him, desire the glory of his kingdom, or pray for grace of the Holy Spirit to do his will. We also ask for "our bread," and thus we pray for the sustenance of our fellow man. We must note that we pray for "daily" bread that is sufficient for the needs of today, not for tomorrow or the next day, but simply for *hodie*. Praying for daily sustenance, however, does not excuse us from our daily labor, even though all things are given to us from God's free bounty.[167]

And forgive us our debts

This and the next two petitions are called deprecations, that is, for the removing of evil. There are three: sins past, sins to come, and the evil of punishment. Again in this petition we pray not only for our forgiveness of past sins but also for those of our brothers. All these sins, as great as they are, God will forgive; he will give us grace to repent so that our lives can be transformed into a state of grace.

---

166. Ibid., pp. 407, 412.
167. Ibid., pp. 413, 415, 421.

We need too to ask for remission for those sins that proceed from some part of us, because they form a partition between God and us; they separate us from God's grace and blessings and hinder our prayers. Andrewes suggested that we should therefore perceive sin like a cloud that prevents our prayers reaching God. So if we do not desire the forgiveness of sins, all other prayers are in vain, as well as excluding us from God's kingdom.

The petition should also remind us that God granted to man something that he did not give to the fallen angels: a chance to repent for the remission of sins.

Hence we should acknowledge ourselves as sinners—indeed, daily sinners—and express out thankfulness for forgiveness of sins. Therefore our comfort is that we continually seek forgiveness from our Father; and as His children, though great sinners, we cannot lose his love and mercy. He is always ready to forgive our sins, be they little or great. Nevertheless, we must strive to die unto sin as Christ died for our sins. This means that we not only confess them, but that we are truly sorry for them and earnestly desire to conquer them.[168]

As we forgive them that trespass against us

In this petition we again show our charity to our neighbor; if we desire God's forgiveness for our sins, we must not only not hate our brother, we must forgive him if he offends us. God wants us to be long-suffering with our brother, just as he is with us. As we run into debt daily with God, we must have the same measure of charity towards others. This is God's way of establishing peace on earth amongst men. If our hearts tell us that we have forgiven our brother, we can be assured that God has forgiven us. By forgiving others we are fitter for God's service, whilst the opposite is also true: if we do not forgive others, we cannot live unto God. If we release our brother, then God releases us.

God has made a covenant with us in that he binds himself to forgive us our sins upon the condition that we forgive others; but if we forgive not, then his covenant is void. It should also remind us that there is a great difference in our forgiving others and God's for-

---

168. Ibid., pp. 424, 430.

giveness of us. Our forgiveness is as a fellow servant, but God is never indebted to us. Forgiveness means forgetting and showing mercy. It is something that we can all do, even the poor, as it costs nothing. [169]

Lead us not into temptation

When we pray these words we are petitioning God to give us the ability to resist sin in the future. If we have asked God to forgive us our sins, we must strive not to sin afresh, and therefore we must strive to overcome the temptations that come to us. It is not enough to confess our sins, to be contrite, or to perform acts of mercy to walk in God's way. We must have a resolute purpose to forsake the sins we have committed and to implement Christ's words, "Go thy way and sin no more." Just as the widow, by the blessing of God, had sufficient oil not only to pay her creditors but also to live, so we must seek of Christ the oil of his grace, both to discharge our sins and to live a holy life.

Furthermore, we must not think ourselves secure when we have received forgiveness of our sins, as illustrated so obviously by the Apostles who, after receiving the Sacrament, which is a seal for remission of sin, committed sin shortly afterwards in the garden. It is when we are cleansed that we are most in danger of subjection by Satan. Thus we need to pray for grace to withstand Satan's temptations. His temptations are quite different from God's; he induces us to sin and draw us away from God, while God afflicts us in order to test our faith. Yet the devil's temptations cannot hurt us if we throw ourselves back on God and his grace.[170]

But deliver us from evil

Here we seek to be delivered from the troubles of this life, expressed in a petition that will continue until the last enemy, death, is destroyed. We pray that God will take from us all those evils that the devil desires us to have in order to ensnare our souls. If we are to be delivered from the power of Satan we must possess the freedom of Christ, who is Wisdom and Power and who will free us from evil.

---

169. Ibid., pp.433,435, 437.
170. Ibid., pp.441- 443.

However we must not confuse our praying to be delivered from evil and our bearing the cross in this life to Calvary, especially when we suffer innocently. We can never live the Christian life without the cross.[171]

For thine is the kingdom, the power and the glory

God's kingdom, so different from an earthly kingdom, is everlasting and universal, and so we pray for that glory which will last forever and ever. Like the Samaritan who returned to give thanks to our Lord, we have a duty to do likewise. Just as this prayer began with a confession of God's goodness, it ends with a confession of God's power as it proclaims the Trinity: Father the glory as king defends his subjects; the Son in conquering death proclaims the kingdom; and the Holy Spirit manifests his power and goodness. It is the duty of subjects to give service to their king, and so when we say the doxology we join with the angels and saints who unceasingly sing of God's honor, power, and glory. [172]

Amen

Andrewes insisted that our duty in saying the Lord's Prayer could not be understood properly unless we comprehend this word correctly. Having made our various petitions to God, we want to be respected by him, as we are of his kingdom and under his jurisdiction. In our "Amen" we ratify all petitions and we confess all glory to God, whose faithfulness is like that of a mother.

We should also say it as an act of thanksgiving in imitation of the angels singing "Amen" to God's praise and honour. God bestows his promises to us when we fittingly conclude this prayer.

The "Amen" must always be said confidently, showing that we look forward to the fulfillment of all the petitions. Yet if we are honest, can we say "Amen" to all them? For example, do we really say "Amen" to saying "yes" to God's will and obeying his commandments, or being led from temptation or to hallow God's holy name?[173]

---

171.   Ibid., pp.454, 456.
172.   Ibid., pp. 460,463.
173.   Ibid., pp.474, 476.

Andrewes, in these sermons, gave us much to ponder on in our daily lives as Christians. The saints of old and not so old tell us that we struggle daily with temptations from Satan, who clearly wants to allure us from God. But Andrewes tells us "Satan is chained by God so that he cannot go further than God will give him leave, which maketh our comfort."[174] For this very prayerful prelate there is never a time or place or situation in which we cannot pray to our heavenly Father, in praise or petition. Let us heed him.

---

174.   Ibid., p. 445.

CHAPTER NINE
THE PERENNIAL CROSS:
GOOD FRIDAY

*It is well known that Christ and His cross
were never parted, but that all His life long
was a continual cross. At the very cratch,
His cross began.*[175]

Tradition tells us that the Christ died on the cross that stood above Adam's grave, and in so doing God restored Adam as a living soul from the dust of the earth. This was his last expression of love after Adam fled and "hid himself in the thick trees." Such was God's love that he eagerly said:

> "Get me a body, I will Myself after Him"... And He gave not over His pursuit, though it were long and laborious, and He full weary; though it cast Him into a "sweat," a "sweat of blood"...through danger, distress, yea, through death itself. Followed, and so followed, as nothing made Him leave following till He overtook.[176]

Adam's sin led to Calvary, and God's love took God to Calvary. Here the two met, and, in the enduring agony that followed, Love absorbed sin into that shattered body as Christ offered up his sinless life to the Father. Thus the passion and death of Christ countered all those sins of Adam. Accordingly, "for the flattering speeches of

---

175.   Ibid., Vol. 2, p. 166.
176.   Ibid., Vol. 1, pp. 6-7.

Adam," Christ "heard all reproaches"; for the beholding of the fruit "which was pleasant in [Adam's] eyes, Christ…was 'buffetted about the eyes'; for Adam's hand stretching out to touch and take the fruit, Christ's hands were stretched out and nailed upon the crosse"; Adam's "eating of this pleasant fruit, was redressed by [Christ's] eating of bitter gall and sharp vinegar." In Adam "we shall dye the death, but Christ has "tasted death for all men." [177]

The Cross, an instrument of torture, became the instrument of love on which Christ, the unblemished lamb, was slain. Using Pascha imagery, Andrewes explained:

> For not only by His death…by the blood of His cross as by the blood of the paschal lamb, the destroyer passeth over us, and we shall not perish; but also by His death, as by the death of our High Priest—for He is Priest and Sacrifice both—we are restored from our exile, even to our former estate in the land of Promise.

Not by the blood of the old covenant but by "the blood of the Testament" are we are given an "estate in that Heavenly inheritance." Although our sins have "deprived us of Paradise, a place on earth…by the purchase of His blood we are entitled to a far higher, even the Kingdom of Heaven." Moreover, by "His blood, not only the blood of 'remission,' to acquit us of our sins, but 'the blood of the Testament' too, to bequeath us and give us estate in that heavenly inheritance."[178]

Therefore at Calvary "we are restored from our exile, even to our former forfeited estate in the land of Promise." Not only is "Christ's death the sacrificial death demanded in justice by His Father, but it is also the blood of the paschal lamb," and therefore "the destroyer passeth over us, and we shall not perish" and even be brought to a far better place "than the estate our sins bereft us." That bequeath from Christ on the Cross is our "heavenly inheritance."[179]

In his lecture on Genesis 4:3, Andrewes maintained that Abel's offering of the lamb was really the forerunner of Christ's. For what else does the cutting of the throat of a lamb or any other beasts symbolise but "the confessions of our sinnes?" "As the Lamb dieth,

---

177.   *Apos. Sacra*, p. 288.
178.   Andrewes, Vol. 2, p. 153.
179.   Ibid., p. 153.

so we deserve the death both of body and soul: And as the Lamb was burnt to ashes; so we deserved to be burnt in the lake of fire and brimstone." That was why Jews and even heathens slaughtered their lambs or other beasts upon their altars. With them, the Church has always confessed "that we cannot have remission of sinnes, without the shedding of blood."

> So the Lambe which *Abel* offered, in the fourth of *Genesis*, which *Esay* forsaw should stand before his shearers, in the fifty third of *Isaiah* whom *John Baptist* pointed at.... *Ecce Agnus Dei* is Christ the Son of God, slain from the beginning of the world, to take away sinnes.[180]

The Cross was undoubtedly the centre of Andrewes' devotional life. "Blessed are the hours that are so spent" in beholding it, he preached. When he delivered his sermons on the Passion it was with the earnest desire to make his auditors participants rather than spectators; he presented the Passion in such realistic terms so that they could see, hear, and feel the agony and sufferings of Christ. "The cross is but a little word, but of great contents," he would say. He believed that if his auditors would only give the time and tenacity to meditate upon Jesus nailed to the cross they would comprehend something of the cost of Love—and would respond to it.[181]

This appeal to the senses in order to aid in meditation was never more apt than at Passiontide, when Christ is presented "to our eye...hanging on the cross" where "our sight then is Jesus, and in Jesus." A crucifix thus makes us "fix our eye, to keep it from straying, to make us look on Him full." Here "our own eyes are witness" to Christ's "bodily suffering." He thus challenged his auditors, "who is there who can look unto those hands and feet, that head and that heart of His that endured all this" and not be moved to tears, unless hearts are made of iron? Even if they are, Andrewes suggested, "They cannot choose but feel the magnetical force of this loadstone. For to a loadstone does He resemble Himself, when He says of Himself, 'Were I once lift up,' *omnia traham ad Me.*" [182]

---

180.   *Apos. Sacra*, pp. 377 - 8.
181.   Andrewes, Vol. 2, pp. 159, 167.
182.   Ibid., pp. 161, 181-2.

If we stay long enough "our very eye will soon tell us no place was left in His body, where He might be smitten and was not." We shall also see that "His skin and flesh rent with the whips and scourges, His hands and feet wounded with the nails, His head with the thorns, His very heart with spear-point; all His senses, all His parts laden with whatsoever wit or malice could invent." Andrewes depicted how "His blessed body" was "given as an anvil to be beaten upon with the violent hands of those barbarous miscreants, till they brought Him into this case of *si fuerit sicut.*" This was such a pitiful sight that Andrewes believed "it would have moved the hardest heart of all to have relented and said, This is enough, we desire no more."[183]

However long we spend contemplating upon the cross, thought Andrewes, we shall never fathom the extent of Christ's soul-suffering. "The sorrows of His soul are unknown sorrows, and for them none ever have…or ever will suffer the like…or near the like in any degree." Indeed, he insisted, "What His feelings were, it is dangerous to define; we know them not, we may be too bold to determine of them." Therefore he believed it was to a

> very good purpose…that the ancient Fathers of the Greek Church in their Liturgy, after they have recounted all the particular pains, as they are set down in His Passion, and by all, and by every one of them, called for mercy, do after all shut up all with this; "By Your unknown sorrows and sufferings, felt by you, but not distinctly known by us, Have mercy upon us, and save us."[184]

Andrewes' constant plea for us to gaze upon the cross was not only that we could soak in the love of God the Son but also as our grateful response to God's immeasurable mercy, which has made us His heirs of His kingdom despite our rebellion. So he begged his auditors to:

> Look upon thy crucified Saviour & love him. He loved thee first, cast an affection upon thee, when thou wast a stranger, nay not a stranger only, but an enimy, an enimy so stubborn, that thou stood out in rebellion, so poor, that thou wast exposed to the

---

183. Ibid., pp. 143-4.
184. Ibid., pp. 144-5.

loathing of thy person, so contemptible that no one pittied thee; and yet when thou wast in such a case, he cast his skirt over thee & made that the time of love.... A man hath nothing more precious then his blood, & that he would & did spend so to espouse us...if you aske me how much I cannot tell. Christ so loved his enimyes, that he made them his friends, so loved sinners, that he made them just men, so the children of wrath, that he made them vessels of mercy, so loved the servants of sin that he would make you his brethren, so the children of darknesse, that he would make you members of his own body, so poor beggars, that he would make them his sons & heirs, heirs of a king[dom], heirs of the king[dom] of Heaven.[185]

Andrewes challenged his auditors to participate in the sufferings of Christ and to recognise that they were responsible for the agonizing death of the Word incarnate. "It was the sin of our polluted hands that pierced His hands, the swiftness of our feet to do evil that nailed His feet, the wicked devices of our heads that gored His head, and the wretched desires of our hearts that pierced His heart."

We cannot thus blame "the Jews and others" who were merely "accessories and instrumental," for "we are, even the principals in this murder." Andrewes insisted that unless our hearts are made of stone they will "melt with compassion" when we confess that he was pierced" by us "wretched sinners." Therefore we must not forget it was for our sins that "the Son of God has His very heart-blood shed forth." [186]

If we fully recognise our part in the agonising death of our Lord, it must needs strike into us remorse of a deeper degree than before; that not only it is we who have pierced the part thus found slain, but that this party, whom we have thus pierced, is not a principal person among the children of men, but even the only-begotten Son of the Most High God. Which will make us cry out with St. Augustine, "Now sure, deadly was the bitterness of our sins, that might not be cured, but by the bitter death and blood-shedding Passion of the Son of God."

---

185.   Ms. 3707, p. 169.
186.   Andrewes, Vol. 2, pp. 126-7, 129.

All this can be gleaned as we look "upon Him."[187]

In encouraging his auditors to meditate on the cross, Andrewes employed mediæval imagery, one of which made popular by St. Bernard was *liber charitatis* (the book of love). When the book is opened we may read the extent of our Saviour's love "in the cleft of His heart." As Bernard expressed it, quoted by Andrewes, "the point of the spear serves us instead of a key, letting us through His wounds see His very heart." It thus revealed a "heart of tender love and most kind compassion, that would for us endure to be so entreated." So it is this piercing of the heart that is crucial in man's redemption, which was very evident in his sermon on Good Friday, 1597, where he portrayed Christ's suffering in hart imagery.

Christ is first the "hart" roused early in the morning by the hunter, as evident in the circumstances following after his birth: "He was by Herod, hunted and chased all His life long." Then "this day [i.e. Good Friday] brought to His end, and, as the poor deer, stricken and pierced through side, heart, and all." Although "his feet, hands and head were pierced," Andrewes emphasised they were not done by "the spear-point." Only his heart felt the "spear-point which pierced, and went through His very heart itself." This was "the deadliest and deepest wound" of them all, which penetrated to his very soul. Andrewes insisted that it is essential to understand how this deep piercing of Christ's heart etched itself on his very soul as well.[188]

For us to comprehend anything of our Lord's passion, the piercing of his heart must prick ours too, and it will, if we allow the spear to "enter past the skin." This will enable us to behold His "heart of compassion and tender love, whereby He would and was content to suffer all this for our sakes." Yet not for us alone but for all "who sought His death." He was content "to be pierced for His piercers." Thus "the more steadily and more often we shall fix our eye upon [the crucifix], the more we shall be inured; and being inured, the more desire to do it." Moreover, "at every looking some new sight will offer itself, which will offer unto us occasion, either of godly sorrow, true repentance, sound comfort, or some other reflection, issuing from the beams of this heavenly mirror." Surely

---

187. Ibid., p. 129.
188. Ibid., pp. 120, 122.

such a viewing will unleash St. Thomas' act of faith, "My Lord and My God." [189]

But Andrewes was not content that this was all that needed to be done. "His grievous passion" is not only for looking and thinking on, but also for doing something. One cannot be a Mary without being a Martha, as contemplation must lead to some active expression of our viewing. He thus posed the question, "Shall we always receive grace, even streams of grace issuing from Him Who is pierced, and shall there not from us issue something back again, that He may look for and receive from us that from Him have, and do daily, receive so many good things?" Undoubtedly, "if love which pierced Him have pierced us aright" we shall give and give generously. Even "if we have nothing to render, yet ourselves to return with the Samaritan, and falling down at His feet, with a loud voice, to glorify His goodness."[190]

However, for Andrewes the most fruitful way to view the Cross is to do what "our Lord commanded, *Hoc facite in commemorationem.*" In the Liturgy "His death is showed forth until He come and the mystery of this His piercing so many ways, so effectually represented before us." This way, we not only behold Christ's crucifixion visually but are also partakers "of his sufferings" whenever we receive his Body and Blood.

Utilizing this sensuous approach, Andrewes suggested that as we receive the Cup, his Blood, for "'the remission of sins,'" we should try to hear the cry of our Saviour from the cross. "Blood...also hath 'a voice,' specially innocent blood, the blood of Abel, that cries loud in God's ears." Yet this is not as "loud as the blood whereof this 'cup of blessing' is 'the communion;' the voice of it will be heard above all, the cry of it will drown any cry else. And as it cries higher, so it differs in this, that it cries in a far other key." Unlike Abel's cry, our Lord cries "not for revenge, but for 'remission of sins'; for that, whereof it is itself the price and purchase, for our salvation in that 'great and terrible day of the Lord,' when nothing else will save us."[191]

---

189. Ibid., pp. 129-131, 133.
190. Ibid., pp. 134-5.
191. Ibid., Vol. 2, p. 134, Vol. 3, p. 321; *Apos. Sacra*, p. 643.

Our viewing the Cross will also enable us to realise that the water and blood that flowed from his pierced side represent, in the words of St. Augustine, the "twin sacraments." Andrewes illustrated this in his 1597 Passion sermon when he stated that Zechariah had preached that "out of His pierced side God 'opened a fountain of water to the House of Israel for sin and for uncleanness'; of the fullness whereof we all have received in the Sacrament of our Baptism." The prophet had called the blood that "blood of the New Testament" which runs "in the high and holy mysteries of the Body and Blood of Christ. There may we be partakers of the flesh of the Morning Hart, as upon this day killed" and receive remission of sins when we are "partakers of the cup of salvation, the precious blood which was shed for the remission of our sins."[192]

If we patiently persevere in our looking "upon Him" and "into Him," and if we stay focused on his grief and love, we shall feel the comfort of his grace swelling within our hearts. Our experience will be similar to that of the two travellers on the road to Emmaus on that first Easter day after they met and conversed with Christ. Our hearts will burn, and above all they will burn with love as we allow "His wounds…[to] heal us, his nakednesse…[to] be cloathing, his shame…[to] be our glorie, his death…[to] be the means to atain our life." The Cross is thus the "eye of our hope."[193]

---

192. Andrewes, Vol. 2, p. 134.
193. Ibid., 134; *Apos. Sacra*, p. 245.

CHAPTER TEN
THE PERENNIAL NOURISHMENT:
THE BLESSED SACRAMENT

The ordaining of His last sacrament, [is]...
the means to re-establish "our hearts
with grace," and to repair the decays of our
spiritual strength; even "His own flesh,
the Bread of life," and "His own blood,
the Cup of salvation."[194]

Andrewes believed it was hardly possible to live the Christian life unless we receive the Sacrament of the Altar regularly, as it is only here that the Christian receives the life of our Lord. That was the main reason for his insistence, but there were others too. These included: union with Christ, renewing our covenant, assurance of the forgiveness of sin, and union with fellow Christians, living and departed.

The high regard that Andrewes had for the Sacrament was evident in this Christmas sermon preached at St. Giles, Cripplegate, his parish church in London (now in the shadow of the Barbican). "We are said to come to Christ in Baptism...in the hearing of the word," and in preaching, "but Christ receiveth none of these, but that we come to him as is *panis vitae*, when we come to Christ, as he offers himself in the Sacrament." Christ gathers "us as close and near as *alimentum alito*, that is as near as near may be." Indeed it is more, for by "that blessed union" it enables us to enter into "the highest per-

---

194.   Andrewes, Vol. 1, p. 169.

fection we can in this life aspire unto." It is then at the altar that our faith is "at the highest; for when we have the body and blood of Christ in our hands, then it makes us say with Thomas.... *Domine mi and Deus mi.*"[195] It is no wonder then that Andrewes, like Greek Fathers such as Basil, advocated frequent communion.[196]

Like the early Fathers, Andrewes believed exactly what our Lord said: "This is my body," "This is my blood," and that the communicant receives Christ's Body and Blood at the Eucharist. This he illustrated in his 1615 Christmas sermon, when he referred to Christ's birthplace not only as happening in the past at Bethlehem but also now at the altar, the perpetual Bethlehem. Unlike the shepherds or wise men, none has to travel to "the town itself," or "go out of this room" because "here is to be had the 'true bread of life that came down from Heaven'...and where that Bread is, there is Bethlehem for ever." Andrewes indicated that was why in the early Church a star was engraved on the canister "wherein was the Sacrament of His body."[197]

This belief was also very evident in his first Christmas sermon preached before James I in 1605, when he affirmed that Christ has taken our flesh, and that on this day we partake of his flesh. By this partaking, the union between Christ and us is closer than that of a wedded couple.

> This day *Verbum caro factum est.* But specially in His flesh as this day gives it, as this day would have us.... Because He has so done, taken ours of us, we also ensuing His steps will participate with Him and with His flesh which He has taken of us. It is most kindly to take part with Him in that which He took part in with us, and that, to no other end, but that He might make the receiving of it by us a means whereby He might "dwell in us, and we in Him." He taking our flesh, and we receiving His Spirit; by His flesh which He took of us receiving His Spirit which He imparts to us; that, as He by ours became *consors humanae naturae,* so we by His might become *consortes Divinae naturae,* "partakers of the

---

195. *Apos. Sacra*, p. 597; Andrewes, Vol. 1, p. 281.
196. Basil stated that "Daily communion and participation in the holy body and blood of Christ is a good and helpful practice." H. Bettensen, Ed. *The Later Christian Fathers* (Oxford, 1989), p. 89.
197. Andrewes, Vol. 1, pp. 173, 247, Vol. 2, p. 362.

Divine nature." Verily, it is the most straight and perfect "taking hold" that is. No union so knits as it. Not consanguinity; brethren fall out. Not marriage; man and wife are severed. But that which is nourished, and the nourishment wherewith—they never are, never can be severed, but remain one for ever. With this act then of mutual "taking," taking of His flesh as He has taken ours, let us seal our duty to Him this day, for taking not "angels," but "the seed of Abraham."[198]

Christmas, Andrewes insisted, is thus a special time to reflect on the Blessed Sacrament, when the Word became flesh. It is indeed inseparable from the altar, as evident in his sermon for Christmas, 1612: "And this day they first came together, the Word and flesh; therefore, of all days, this day they would not be parted." Two years later he concluded his Nativity sermon with this commendation: "This then I commend to you, even the being with Him in the Sacrament of His Body—that Body that was conceived and born, as for the other ends so for this specially, to be "with you"; and this day, as for other intents, so even for this, for the Holy Eucharist."[199] It is not surprising that most of his sermons given at the Royal Court ended with the interweaving of the particular festival with receiving Christ at the celebration of the Eucharist. Of course, it was his Nativity sermons that especially expressed this union when we celebrate "the Word became flesh." Hence he concluded his 1610 sermon:

> Let us honour this day with our receiving, which He has honoured by His first giving; yielding Him evermore...our unfeigned hearty thanksgiving for this so good news, for this so great a gift, both of them this day [given to] us; in Him and for Him, Who was Himself the gift, our "Saviour, Christ the Lord."[200]

In his Paschal sermons Andrewes emphasised how the Passover Supper anticipated the Supper of the Lamb, which will be a per-

---

198. Ibid., Vol. 1, pp. 16 –7.
199. Ibid., pp. 116, 151 – 2.
200. Ibid., p. 84.

petual feast of joy. Undoubtedly Christians are the happiest of all people "in this valley of tears."

> There is a further matter…for as this feast looks back as a memorial of that is already past and done for us, so does it look forward, and is to us a pledge of another and a better yet to come, the feast of the marriage of the Lamb here who is our Passover, where whosoever shall be a guest, the angels pronounce him happy and blessed for ever.

> That is the last and great feast indeed, when all destroyers and all destructions will cease and come to an end for evermore, and we hear that joyful voice, *Transi in gaudium Domini, Passover into the joy of the Lord*, the joys of heaven, joys not mingled with any sour leaven as this world's joy is, but pure and entire; not transient as that of this world, and ever flitting and forsaking us then soonest when we think we have best hold of them, but permanent and abiding still. A Passover that will never be passed over, but last and continue as feast to all eternity. Of that, this here is a pledge, if we neglect it not as it were not worth the taking. And He who at this time gave us this pledge, in His good time also bring us to the Passover whereof this is the pledge, even to the never-passing but everlasting joys and happiness, of His heavenly kingdom, through the offering of His blessed Son the very Paschal Lamb![201]

Calvary and the altar are also inseparable. At Calvary, Christ's death was made "the medicine," of which "the Water and the Blood" flowing from His wounded side were "to be the ingredients" for what Augustine described as the "twin sacraments." Andrewes illustrated this in his 1597 Passion sermon when he took Zechariah's words (13:1) that "out of His pierced side God 'opened a fountain of water to the House of Israel for sin and for uncleanness;' of the fullness whereof we all have received in the Sacrament of our Baptism." Of "'the blood of the New Testament' we may receive this day; for it will run in the high and holy mysteries of the Body and Blood of Christ. There may we be partakers of the flesh of the Morning Hart, as upon this day killed. There may we be partakers

---

201.   Ibid., Vol. 2, p. 308.

of the cup of salvation, the precious blood which was shed for the remission of our sins."[202]

Andrewes considered the Word of God and the Word in the Sacrament to be inseparable:

> To go to the word and flesh together.... But at this now, we are not to content ourselves with one alone; but since He offers to communicate Himself both ways, never restrain Him to one. The word we hear is the abstract of *Verbum*; the Sacrament is the antetype of *caro*, His flesh. What better way than where these are actually joined, actually to partake them both? Not either alone, the word or flesh; but the word and flesh both, for there they are both.... If it be grace and truth we respect, how may we better establish our hearts with grace, or settle our minds in the truth of His promise, than by partaking these the conduit-pipes of His grace, and seals of His truth unto us? Grace and truth now proceeding not from the Word alone, but even from the flesh thereto united; the fountain of the Word flowing into the cistern of His flesh, and from thence deriving down to us this grace and truth, to them who partake Him aright. [203]

Like the early Fathers, Andrewes stressed the unifying nature of the Sacrament. It is the "Sacrament of peace and unity," he preached, and therefore the Eucharist should ideally be the meeting place for all Christians. It is "for all sorts," Andrewes insisted, but nothing had divided his contemporaries, as it still does today, as much as Christ's Body and Blood. Yet at the Liturgy God's people gather together for prayers and for "the dispensation of His holy mysteries," That gathering should reflect "the symbols of many grains into the [bread]...and many grapes into the [wine]," which is completed at the altar where "we gather Christ Himself." The importance of coming together as one, Andrewes pointed out, is reflected in one of the names given for the Eucharist in the early Church: *Synaxis*.[204]

This concern for unity was particularly evident in some of his sermons at St. Giles. In one of these he compared the fraction of

---

202.   Ibid., p. 134, Vol. 3, p. 113.
203.   Ibid, pp. 101 – 1.
204.   Ibid., Vol. 1, pp. 281 - 2.

Christ's body with that which Paul addressed in the Corinthian Church. With the latter, Andrewes stated that St. Paul had appealed to the schismatic and contentious at Corinth to live in "love and concord" with one another. Paul's reason for pressing unity was that they were all "one body" in Christ who is the head and only source of every Christian's "one beginning and one nourishment." That beginning is "in the fountain of regeneration" when we are "baptized into one body by one spirit, and all made to drink of one spirit." After that Christians come together in "the Sacrament of accord." Such accord was seen in the Apostles as they broke bread together and "in the many grains kneaded into 'one loaf,' and the many grapes pressed into one cup," a quotation from Cyprian, used by Andrewes and many other theologians of his day. This unity is also demonstrated at the fraction, when Christ's body is broken for all, and, as St. Paul said, "We are all 'one bread and one body, so many as are partakers of one bread.'" This makes it the *"locus* of unity." Furthermore, as the two natures in Christ are "united together," so in the Sacrament all Christians should be united. Like St. Paul, Andrewes insisted that if Christians could be persuaded they are partakers of the one Body of Christ and members of that Body, then "there would not be such divisions and dissensions in the World as they are." Andrewes always maintained that we cannot ideally participate in the Sacrament unless we earnestly desire union with one another, thereby making our participation active rather than passive, as Christians are meant to be "living stones" in that "body mystical" by growing in "mutual love and charity."[205]

At a time when the Calvinist doctrine of predestination abounded, Andrewes preached incessantly on the universality of redemption and grace. Never is Andrewes' universalism clearer than in his Eucharistic teaching. In a sermon delivered at St. Giles in 1599 he stressed that all who come to Christ receive Christ, despite what they are. No one is excluded from his banquet because we are all sinners. "We come to Christ, as he offers himself in the Sacrament to be the lively food of our souls." Christ will not "cast out" any who come, but rather he will be "received to be a member of Christs mystical body, 'and partaker of the divine nature.'" He also

---

205.   Ibid., p. 282, Vol. 2, p. 289; *Apos. Sacra*, p. 614; Cyprian, *The Epistles Of S. Cyprian*, L.F. Vol. 17 (Oxford: J. H. Parker, 1844), p. 161 (lxiii.10).

taught that if ever we are going to be "contrite and broken in spirit" it is in the context of the Eucharist. Of course, another reason for sinners to come to the Sacrament is to receive "active grace" in order to resist sin, to endure "the conflict of sinne, and to be conquerors over Satan and own our corruptions." Andrewes also emphasised that the ancient Fathers had noted that there is "no unworthinesse by means of any filth, either of body or soul," that will keep Christ "from us." In his incarnate life Christ showed for "bodily uncleannesse, he was content to be received by Simon the leper...and...in regard of spirituall pollution...Christ...doth not only receive sinners, but 'eats with them.'" Thus sinners are assured that Christ not only eats with them "but receives them into that union, that is, to be one with him; which is a greater union that is either between brother and brother or between man and wife." Another assurance is that at Calvary Christ "was content to receive the thief," and he also prayed "'Father forgive them.'" "Therefore it is most likely that he will receive us, if we come to him." As the Fathers also emphasised, the only condition is "that we come."[206]

What if the communicant comes and is an unrepentant sinner? Andrewes did not explicitly say, except that the sinner still receives "the body and blood" of our Lord, but he implies that it is to his damnation. And what of those who do not come? Though they deserve to be cast out, Andrewes believed that "yet Christ doth not cast them out, but they cast out themselves, in as much as they sever themselves from this Sacrament and from the memorial of his loving kindness." He insisted that those who do not come to the Eucharist are heathenish, no better than Jews and Turks. If they want to "be bidden to the Lambs Supper" then it is imperative they "come to the Lords Supper," but if they "neglect the opportunity, they shall be cast out, as Saul was." It also reflects another of his favorite Pauline themes, though "sin abounds, grace superabounds."

---

206. *Apos. Sacra*, pp. 596 - 7, 601. He preached in a similar vein in his first Christmas sermon at the Jacobean court. Verily, it is the most straight and perfect 'taking hold' that is. No union so knitteth as it. Not consanguinity; brethren fall out. Not marriage; man and wife are severed. But that which is nourished, and the nourishment wherewith - they never are, never can be severed, but remain one for ever. Andrewes, Vol. 1, pp. 16 - 7.

Providing they show some contrition, Christians coming to Christ in the Sacrament are assured of forgiveness when they receive the cup of Salvation. When our lips touch "the cup of blessing" our sins are purged, bringing healing and forgiveness. We must therefore never underestimate the power of God that in Christ "our sins shall be taken away by the outward act of the sacrament." Just as the Sacrament is for sinners, it is also the remedy against sin; it is the antidote against the wiles of Satan, as it assures us that Christ as "the seed of the woman" has vanquished "the seed of the Serpent." [207]

When Andrewes preached on covenantal theology (another favorite Reformation theology) it was always from a sacramental approach. Our covenant with God is made in baptism, the first seal. But as this covenant is constantly broken by sin, it has to be renewed just as constantly. This is done by receiving the Blessed Sacrament, the second seal. "We know the Sacrament is the seal of the new covenant, as it was of the old. Thus, by undertaking the duty He requires, we are entitled to the comfort which here He promises. And do this He would have us, as is plain by His *hoc facite*." Therefore:

> [A]ll the times in our life, when we settle ourselves to prepare thitherwards, we are in best terms of disposition to covenant with Him. For if ever we be in a state of love towards Him, or towards one another, then it is. If ever troubled in spirit, that we have not kept His commandments better, then it is. If ever in a vowed purpose and preparation better to look to it, then it is. Then therefore of all times most likely to gain interest in the promise, when we are best in case, and come nearest to be able to plead the condition.[208]

Receiving the Blessed Sacrament restores man to his rightful nature, which Andrewes taught in another of his favorite images, "the tree of life." Adam, by being cast out of the garden, was "kept from the tree of life," the original sacrament, but was restored with the second Adam. Christ restored the original purpose of the tree in the garden to give eternal life, and now, unlike Adam, we are not barred from that "tree of life" which is freely given by partaking in

---

207. *Apos. Sacra*, pp. 519 - 20, 600, 624, 683.
208. Andrewes, Vol. 3, p. 161.

the life of the second Adam. Christ "is a Paradise of all joyes and happinesse."

"By eating the flesh of Christ, the first fruits of life" we overcome death in the "first Adam" by becoming "branches of the Vine." Hence we are "partakers of His nature, and so of His life and verdure both." That Sacrament is the dispenser of life, life from "the fruit of the Tree in Paradise" as well as life from the Living Bread—that is the flesh of Son of God. All this Christ has promised, providing we are faithful; if not, like Adam we shall be forbidden entrance by the angel holding a "fierie sword." This means we must "strive to overcome...every temptation." When we fall from grace "we obtain victory again sinne and death by the blood of the Lamb, being drunk in the Sacrament."[209]

One of his favorite texts in his teaching on participation was from St. John's discourse on *"I am the Bread of Heaven"*. Accordingly in a sermon at St. Giles', he taught that we were *"to Labour not for that bread which perisheth* but *Labour for that which endureth;"* the first kind cannot endure for long before it perishes, but the bread for the soul never does. It never perishes because "it is Christ, *the Sonne of man, that gives us this bread of life"*. "Therefore it stands us upon to come to Christ, that he may receive us to be one with him in the life of grace, and partakers with him in his kingdom of glory." We must never forget that Our Lord "commands us not only to seek and desire in our hearts" this everlasting Bread, "but to hunger for it as we doe for the food of our bodies."[210]

Another of Andrewes' favorite themes during his ministry was *theosis*, that is, man becoming like God. The main way to become Godlike was to receive Christ's body and blood. "He is in us and we in him, we and Christ are made one, we receive him and he receives us: So that as God cannot hate Christ, so he cannot but love us, being engrafted into him." Through the Sacrament we are absorbed into His nature. Andrewes saw the fraction as the visual teaching of the fusing of the divine and the human.

Now "the bread which we break, is it not the partaking of the body, of the flesh, of Jesus Christ?" It is surely, and by it and by

---

209. Ibid., Vol. 2, p. 220; *Apos. Sacra*, pp. 573 - 4.
210. Ibid., pp. 531, 534, 537, 601.

nothing more are we made partakers of this blessed union... Because He hath so done, taken ours of us, we also ensuing His steps will participate with Him and with His flesh which He hath taken of us. It is most kindly to take part with Him in that which He took part in with us, and that, to no other end, but that He might make the receiving of it by us a means whereby He might "dwell in us, and we in Him."

His *theosis* teaching mirrored that of the Orthodox Church. Gregory of Nyssa had taught that "He disseminates Himself in every believer through that flesh, whose existence comes from bread and wine, blending Himself with the body of believers, to secure that, by this union, with the immortal, man, too, may be sharer in incorruption." A few centuries later Gregory Palamas wrote, "[By] partaking of the body and blood of His humanity, we receive God Himself in our souls—the Body and Blood of God."[211]

The Sacrament is also the source of comfort in our pilgrimage to the Supper of the Lamb. Andrewes explicitly taught in his 1610 Pentecost sermon how the Church teaches us that that Sacrament was ordained for "our comfort," for we hear it read so often: "He hath ordained these mysteries of His love and favour, to our great and endless comfort," and "The Father shall give you the Comforter." That Comforter is Christ, and so "by the flesh we eat, and the blood we drink at His table, we be made partakers of His Spirit, and of the comfort of it." The comfort we receive can be ascertained in that bread itself strengthens or makes strong, and comfort means "to make strong," while wine cheers and gladdens the heart and therefore comforts those who "mourn and are oppressed with grief." The outward symbols "show that the same effect is wrought in the inward man by the holy mysteries...that there the heart is 'established by grace, and our soul endued with strength, and our conscience made light and cheerful, that it faint not, but evermore rejoice in His holy comfort."[212]

Andrewes continues:

---

211. Andrewes, Vol. 1, p. 16; *Apos. Sacra*, p. 600; J. Meyendorff, *Byzantium Theology* (New York, 1983). pp. 201, 205.
212. Andrewes, Vol. 3, pp. 161 - 2.

Besides, it was one special end why the Sacrament itself was ordained, our comfort; the Church so tells us, we so hear it read every time to us: "He hath ordained these mysteries of His love and favour, to our great and endless comfort. The Father will give you the Comforter." Why He gives Him, we see; how He gives Him, we see not. The means for which He gives Him, is Christ—His entreaty by His word in prayer; by His flesh and blood in sacrifice, for His blood speaks, not His voice only. These means for which; and the very same, the means by which He gives the Comforter: by Christ the Word, and by Christ's body and blood, both. In tongues it came, but the tongue is not the instrument of speech only but of taste, we all know...that not only by the letter we read, and the word we hear, but by the flesh we eat, and the blood we drink at His table, we be made partakers of His Spirit, and of the comfort of it.[213]

So it is "in this Sacrament we have both a means of victory and a pledge of our reward, that is, the life of grace begun in us here, to assure us of a glorious life in the world to come." Just as "every tree must have a root," so Christ speaks of the Sacrament being a root when it is sown "in the hearts of the receivers." In time, through the work of the Holy Spirit, it "shoots forth and becomes a tree," giving "a life of grace." This "life of grace" will bestow upon us, when our bodies are raised up from "the dust of death," "the life of glory" in "the heavenly Paradise." In this sense, the Sacrament, for Andrewes, forms a bridge between "the Church Militant" and "the Church Triumphant."[214]

---

213. Ibid.
214. *Apos. Sacra*, pp. 576 - 7.

CHAPTER ELEVEN
THE PERENNIAL SPRING:
EASTER

Nothing is more beautiful as Spring
When weeds in wheel, shoot long and lovely and lush;
Thrush's eggs look little low heavens, and thrush
Through the echoing timber does so rinse and wring
The ear, it strike like lightnings to hear him sing;
The glassy peartree leaves and blooms, they brush
With richness; the racing lambs too have fair their fling.[215]

In the octet of this sonnet, Hopkins captured not only the beauty but also the vibrancy and vitality of spring. He echoes what Lancelot Andrewes had preached long before him: "All things generate anew; the soil of winter is gone, and of summer is not yet come." He assured us it is God who makes "all our gardens green, sends us yearly the spring, and all the herbs and flowers we then gather." Thus spring at its very best is like a painting, and we rejoice in the handiwork of the Artist. Yet, it is all too brief—the loveliness fades and eventually dies, as we know from our Eastertide flowers. However, such loveliness and lushness can be ours forever, for there is such a spring that lasts forever. This is the heavenly spring where "nothing fades, but all springs fresh and green." For such "'an inheritance, blessed be God.'"[216]

---

215. Oscar Williams, Ed. *The Mentor Book of Major British Poets* (New York, 1963), p. 350.
216. Andrewes, Vol. 3, pp. 15 - 6.

Just as there can be no spring without winter, there can be no resurrection without death. The stark, death-like appearance of gardens, meadows and parks in winter reminds us that there can be no life without nakedness. Likewise Christ was stripped of every shred of dignity and honor before he shed his blood. He is the true naked branch, which in due time will explode with life in all its freshness and greenery. Andrewes presented in spring imagery that wonderful, triumphant news of Easter, of Christ "trampling down death by death, and upon those in the tombs bestowing life." Christ "made such a herb grow out of the ground this day as the like was never seen before, a dead body to shoot forth alive out of the grave."[217]

After the broken body of Christ was taken from the Cross, embraced by His blessed Mother, and lovingly embalmed, it was placed tenderly in the tomb in a garden "wherein the ground was in all her glory, fresh and green and full of flowers." During those three days in the "heart of the earth" there was "life in it" when Christ preached to the souls in Hades, and released Adam and all mankind before him. Christ's time there was like "the earth dead for a time, all the winter." However:

> When the waters of heaven fall on [this], shows it has life, bringing forth herbs and flowers again. And even so, when the waters above the heavens, and namely the dew of this day distilling from Christ's rising, will in like sort drop upon it..."as the dew of the herbs, and the earth will give forth her dead."

Andrewes compared Christ's time in the "heart of the earth" with the three days Jonah spent in the belly of the whale. When Jonah was cast up "on dry land" it was the sign for "Christ's arising out of His sepulchre," "from death to life immortal."[218]

Returning to Hopkin's sonnet, we see that the sextet explains that the perfection of spring was also man's, before he sinned and was cast out of paradise:

> What is all this juice and all this joy?
> A strain on the earth's sweet being in the beginning
> In Eden garden—Have get, before it cloy,

---

217. Ibid., p.16.
218. Ibid., Vol. 2, p. 385.

Before it cloud, Christ, lord, and sour with sinning
Innocent mind and Mayday in girl and boy,
Most, O maid's child, thy choice and worth the winning.

That perfection is once again possible for us as the "maid's child," breaking the bond of death has restored the "Eden garden." Nevertheless, we children of Eve, through lack of faith, continually ask, Where may this be, this perfect spring? As frail creatures in this valley of tears we know only this: "It is not here—upon earth no such seat, All here savour of the nature of the soil, *corrumpi, contaminari, marcescere*, are the proper passions of earth, and all earthly things." After Adam's sinning in the Garden of Eden that perennial spring was lost and made unobtainable for us. However, through God's infinite love and mercy the second Adam assures us of another garden, another paradise, even better than the first— Heaven, from where the Word had come to give us this Eden. By living in obedience to his Father's will, Christ absorbed the disobedience of the first Adam into his crucified body and took it back to Heaven. Here nothing is now defiled, "all things keep and continue to this day in their first estate, the original beauty they ever had."[219]

We too can hither ascend to that perfection through his death and rising. Christ not only offers us the heavenly garden, he is the perpetual gardener as well. A dedicated gardener knows how to dig out weeds that choke growth and bloom, and so does the Risen Christ who continually weeds the gardens of our souls and looks after them by watering "them with the dew" in order to bring forth flowers of grace. Andrewes assured us that it is not only our souls that he tends, but also our bodies. He will "turn all our graves into garden-plots," with the firm assurance that "one day [He will] turn land and sea and all into a great garden, and so husband them, as they shall in due time bring forth live bodies, even all our bodies alive again."[220]

This eternal garden is the gift of the Resurrection of Christ. Just as the beginning of spring heralds the certainty of life and loveliness ahead, so does the Resurrection. This brings hope to hearts that have been imprisoned by death and sin: "The hope of that life

219. Ibid., p. 380.
220. Ibid., pp. 376; Vol.3, p.16.

immortal is the very life of this life mortal." Yet the good news that Andrewes related is that we do not have to wait until we have died to experience the eternal life; Christ's resurrection enables us to enjoy our "inheritance" now. The resurrection gives grace; "this day it has an efficacy continuing, that shows forth itself."[221] Or as he preached in another sermon, the Resurrection is the foundation of our faith:

> Of all that be Christians, Christ is the hope; but not Christ every way considered, but as risen. Even in Christ unrisen there is no hope. Well does [St. Paul] begin here; and when he would open to us "a gate of hope," carry us to Christ's sepulchre empty; to show us, and to hear the angels say, "He is risen." Then after to deduce; if He were able to do thus much for Himself, He has promised us as much, and will do as much for us. We shall be restored to life.[222]

One of the features and joys of spring is the melodious sound of the birds. "Where are the songs of spring, aye where are they?" asks the poet. They are everywhere, filling every tree, every bush, and every glade. Similarly, Andrewes suggested that Easter proclaims her special melody to the world with her *Benedictus* of the resurrection of Christ and our benefits from it. In an Easter sermon with its text from St. Peter's first letter, *"Benedictus Deus et Pater Domini nostri Jesu Christi"* [Blessed be the God and Father of our Lord Jesus Christ], Andrewes described this special spring song. Just as there is Zachariah's *Benedictus* for Christmas, there is St. Peter's for Easter, "the proper *Benedictus* for this feast." It is the *Benedictus* for all these and "the means for all: the rising of Christ, this day's work, the dew of this new birth, the gate of this hope, the pledge of this inheritance. For these, owe we this *Benedictus* to God. And this day are we to pay it, every one of us.... Blessed be God. Yes, blessed, and thanked, and praised; *Benedictus, magnificat, jubilate,* and all."[223]

Furthermore, Andrewes encouraged us to have our own *Benedictus* song, but he suggested it could never be long enough to

---

221.   Ibid., p. Vol. 2. 374; Vol. 3, p. 100.
222.   Ibid., Vol. 2, p. 209.
223.   Ibid., pp. 364 - 6.

express all the benefits we have received from Christ's resurrection—and for all his mercies. These are,

> rather *multa*, than *magna*; a word of number, rather than magnitude.... No single mercy would do it—no, though great, there must be many. For many the defects to be removed, many the sins to be forgiven, many the perfections to be attained; therefore, "according to His manifold mercy."

Andrewes implored us to "make much of [mercy] while we live, never pass by it but say it, say it as often as we can; 'blessed be God,' blessed be His mercy...'Blessed be He for His mercy; yes, many times blessed for His manifold mercies.'"[224]

The Benedictus of St. Peter also "gives us a little overture," and it is so conditioned that we "know it is worth a Benedictus." It orchestrates "an inheritance, blessed be God." This inheritance is incorruptible and pure, mirroring spring with its freshness and loveliness, not the end of summer when flowers fade and die—the earthly inheritance. Indeed, in earthly "inheritances there [are] great odds, [often] one much better than another." However, the heavenly inheritance is not only the best but also the same for all, the perennial spring.[225]

The tune also tells us we are "'heirs under hope' till the appointed time" when we shall attain "the 'inheritance' itself." "The resurrection is placed in the midst, between our hope and our inheritance.... So from the estate of hope, by the resurrection as by a bridge, pass we over to the enjoying our inheritance." This comes "not of ourselves, or by our merits...but of Him, and by His mercies," otherwise it would be "a purchase, and no inheritance. It comes to us freely, as the inheritance to children." "At this time, the time of Christ's resurrection, and of our celebrating it, 'to hope' as to the blossom or blade, rising now in the spring; to the 'inheritance'— that, as the crop or fruit to come after at harvest, and the 'harvest' of this crop, says our Saviour, 'is the end of the world.'"[226]

---

224. Ibid., pp. 370 -1.
225. Ibid., pp. 370, 377 -79.
226. Ibid., pp. 365, 376.

Birds fill the air with melodious sounds, but blossoms fill it with sweet smells and sights. The blossoms of spring do more than grace our senses, they assure us that trees will produce a harvest of plenty. In other words they bear "good works." Andrewes also spoke of the Resurrection in terms of "good works" by Christ's rising from the dead. This should even inspire those "who were dead before to good works...to revive...the doing of them." Indeed, the Resurrection is only manifested in us through our fruit of good works. "As there is a reviving, in the earth, when all and every herbs and flowers are 'brought again from the dead,'" so likewise "good works" should come to life "among men [so]...that we be not found fruitless at our bringing back from the dead, in the great Resurrection." Of course, for this divine "every day be for every good work, to do His will."[227]

Andrewes, like Hopkins, often referred to nature as a teacher of the Christian faith. He advised us to go out into the fields and "see how the same corn that lay dead under the clod, sprouts forth, 1st the blade, then the ear, after that full corn." Surely it teaches us that our dead bodies will rise in similar fashion to that abode where "nothing fades, but all springs fresh and green."[228]

---

227.   Ibid., Vol. 3, pp. 83, 102.
228.   Ms. 3707, p. 149.

CHAPTER TWELVE
THE PERENNIAL POWER: PENTECOST

Which we yearly hold holy in thankful
remembrance of the Holy Ghost, promised
to be sent, and sent.[229]

It fills the Church of God; it fills
The sinful world around;
Only in stubborn hearts and wills
No place for it is found. [230]

Nothing can contain the Spirit; it blows where it will and fills not only the Church but also the whole world, renewing, regenerating, and rejuvenating everything in it from day one. One of the misconceptions about the Spirit, according to Andrewes, was that it had been inactive until Pentecost. Nothing is further from the truth. Absolutely nothing has ever been exempted from his power. Hopkins expressed this idea in these lines:

The whole word is charged with the grandeur of God.
It will flame out, like shining from shook foil;
It gathers to a greatness, like the ooze of oil
Crushed.[231]

---

229. Andrewes, Vol. 3, p. 145.
230. J. Keble, *The Christian Year*, (Oxford, 1827), p. 118.
231. G. M. Hopkins, *The Poetical Works of Gerard Manley Hopkins*, ed. R. Bridges (London, 1918), p. 26.

Following in the early Fathers' footsteps, one of Andrewes' favorite descriptions of the Holy Spirit was "breath," which emphasised the giving of life to everything at the beginning of creation. It was not only "*dixit Deus*...the Word, but *ferabatur Spiritus*, the motion of the Spirit, to give the spirit of life."[232]

When God made man he was not only the Potter who moulded him in his image, but also the Glass Maker who sealed that image with his indwelling. "By breathing into Adam, the Father gave the soul, the Author of life natural; the Son...by breathing gives the Holy Spirit, the Author of life spiritual." Yet it is more than just breathing *upon*, it is breathing *into* man: "This *in* shows it pertains within, to the inward parts, to the very conscience...thither goes this breath, and thither is farther than man can go."[233]

Every man in his natural state has been given "breath or inspiration." This is known as natural grace. However, this grace is not sufficient for him to perceive "the things of God" and to "come to the life of glory." For that he needs the supernatural grace given and received in "the waters of Baptism."

"*Accipite Spiritum*, gives to man the life of nature; *Accipite Spiritum Sanctum*, to the Christian man, the life of grace." Andrewes summed up the "correspondence between the natural and the spiritual" this way: "The same way the world was made in the beginning, by the Spirit moving upon the waters of the deep, the very same was the world new-made, the Christian world, or Church, by the same Spirit moving on the waters of baptism."[234]

Moreover, the effectiveness of the Holy Spirit in Baptism can be learned by observing nature. Here "water, if it be not *aqua viva*, have not a spirit to move it and make it run, it stands and putrifies." It is the spirit or quickening that makes the water a well, "springing up to eternity." During Baptism the water washes the "soil from our skin," but it is only through the Holy Spirit that the "stain from our soul" is removed. Therefore there is "no 'laver of regeneration' without 'renewing of the Holy Ghost.'"[235]

---

232. Andrewes, Vol. 3, p. 169.
233. Ibid., p. 271; *Apos. Sacra.* p. 184.
234. Andrewes, Vol. 3, pp. 191, 266.
235. Ibid., pp. 170, 355.

Needless to say, after Baptism the Holy Spirit is often hindered from working in us by our sins. The Spirit is therefore also needed to eradicate sin "if ever it will rightly be put away, the spirit to be searched, and inward hearty compunction wrought there." In one of his loveliest Pentecost sermons, Andrewes spoke of Christ's gift of forgiveness as the breath of the Holy Spirit, breathing on penitents as gently as the dissipating mist in order to dispel sin. In his breath the Spirit counters the breath of the serpent. It was a breath, a "pestilent breath of the serpent, that blew upon our first parents, infected [and] poisoned them at the first," but now at Pentecost it is "Christ's breath" through the Holy Spirit.[236]

Commenting on the appropriateness of "breath" for forgiving sin, Andrewes stated that so often men "are lost in" "a mist or fog" and "blown away" or hardened like "a frost." But by "this breath" it is as it were "to resolve the frost first and turn it into vapour, and after it is so, then to blow it away." Andrewes emphasised that only Christ's breath can "thaw a frost, or scatter a mist," as "the soil of sin is so baked on men, they so hard frozen in the dregs of it, our wind cannot dissolve it." "It is from the breath of His mouth virtue goes" and before it "sin cannot stand," as it is blown "away like a little dust."[237]

Therefore, after Baptism the breath of the Holy Spirit continues to sustain us all our lives:

> By Him after, confirmed in the imposition of hands. By Him after, renewed to repentance, "when we fall away," by a second imposition of hands. By Him taught all our life long that we know not, put in mind of what we forget, stirred up in what we are dull, helped in our prayers, relieved in "our infirmities," comforted in our heaviness; in a word, "sealed to the day of our redemption," and "raised up again in the last day."[238]

Easter may be the queen of all feasts, but without Pentecost other festivals would not be observed, declared Andrewes. It is the linchpin for all Christian festivals. "All the feasts hitherto...from His

---

236. Ibid., pp. 266, 272.
237. Ibid., pp. 266-9.
238. Ibid., p. 191.

Incarnation to the very last of His Ascension, though all of them be great and worthy of all honour in themselves, yet to us they are as nothing, any of them or all of them, even all the feasts in the Calendar, without this day, the feast which now we hold holy to the sending of the Holy Spirit." The Holy Spirit is indeed both the Alpha and Omega in man's process of salvation, beginning "at the Annunciation, when He descended upon the Blessed Virgin, whereby the Son of God did take our nature, the nature of man" and ending "in His descending this day upon the sons of men, whereby they actually become 'partakers of His nature, the nature of God.'" Thus at Pentecost "the Spirit of God first set His seal upon the Fathers of our faith, the blessed Apostles. On which He then did, and on which He ever will, though not in like manner yet in like effect, it being His own way."[239]

Pentecost thus celebrates the "dedication of Christ's Catholic Church on earth," as well as "proclaiming the Apostles' commission" who first published the Gospel. On that day he came "to take the charge, and to establish an order in the Church," and to set his seal upon it.[240]

It is through Christ's Church, stated Andrewes, that the Spirit conveys God's Truth. "From Christ It comes, if It be true; He breathes It. It cannot but be true, if It come from Him, for He is 'the Truth' [but] if it savour of falsehood or folly, it came not from Him, He breathed it not. But His breath shall not fail, shall ever be able to serve His Church." It is the Holy Spirit who must "govern the Church." The only place to receive this Spirit therefore is in "the Sanctuary, and to no other place."[241]

The concept of the Church as Christ's sanctified body was well-illustrated, Andrewes believed, in the speaking of tongues and the appearance of fire at Pentecost:

> The seat of the tongue is in the head, and the "Head of the Church" is Christ. The native place of heat, the quality in us answering to this fire, is the heart, and the heart of the Church is the Holy Spirit. These two join to this work, Christ to give the tongue, the Holy Spirit to put fire into it. [242]

---

239.   Ibid., pp. 108, 145-6, 202.
240.   Ibid., pp. 110, 379.
241.   Ibid., p. 276.
242.   Ibid., p. 124.

This could not have happened if Christ had not ascended. That is why, as Andrewes emphasised, Christ told his disciples, "It is expedient I be gone.... The corporal therefore to be removed, that the spiritual might take place; the visible, that the invisible; and they, not in sight or sense as hitherto, but in spirit and truth henceforth to cleave unto Him."[243]

Indeed, the Spirit was inseparable from Christ during his whole life and ministry, beginning with his conception:

> When He came as Jesus, the Spirit conceived Him. When He came as Christ, the Spirit anointed Him. When He came in water at His Baptism, the Spirit was there; "came down in the shape of a dove, rested, abode on Him." When He came in blood at His Passion, there too. It was "the eternal Spirit of God, by which He offered Himself without spot unto God."[244]

Without the Holy Spirit even Christ's Resurrection and Ascension were incomplete.

> If the Holy Spirit come not, Christ's coming can do us no good; when all is done, nothing is done. No? Said not He *consummatum est*? Yes, and said it truly in respect of the work itself; but *quod nos*, "in regard of us" and making it ours, *non consummatum est*, if the Holy Spirit come not too...if the Seal come not too, nothing is done.[245]

Furthermore, the teachings of Christ, even though he "is the Word," remained "but words spoken or words written" until Pentecost:

> There is no seal put to till this day; the Holy Spirit is the seal or signature, *in Quo signati estis*.... In all of these of Christ's there is but the purchase made and paid for, and as they say, *jus ad rem* acquired; but *jus in re, missio in possessionem*, livery and seizin, that is reserved till this day; for the Spirit is the *Arrha*, "the earnest" or the investiture of all that Christ has done for us. [246]

243. Ibid., pp. 172-3.
244. Ibid., p. 354.
245. Ibid., p. 169.
246. Ibid., p. 108.

What Andrewes was stressing here was that without Pentecost, with its abundant outpouring of the Spirit, the redemptive work of Christ cannot continue; it remains in the past tense. "It is so. For all He hath done, redemption or no redemption goeth by this seal; all that Christ has wrought for us, by that Holy Ghost doth work in us."[247]

This teaching of Andrewes was reflected in an address given in 1968 by the Metropolitan Ignatius of Latakia:

Without the Holy Spirit God is far away.
    Christ stays in the past,
    the Gospel is simply an organization.
    authority is a matter of propaganda,
    the liturgy is no more than an evolution,
    Christian loving a slave morality.
But in the Holy Spirit
    the cosmos is resurrected and grows
    with the birth pangs of the Kingdom,
    the Risen Christ is there,
    the Gospel is the power of life,
    the Church shows forth the life of the Trinity,
    authority is a liberating science,
    mission is a Pentecost,
    the liturgy is both renewal and anticipation,
human action is deified.[248]

Pentecost is also the feast connected with the harvests of spring. Andrewes explained that, under the Old Covenant, this festival was the offering of the first fruits, and so it signified the beginning of the harvest when "they first put their sickle to the corn." Under the New Covenant it now signifies the beginning of "the great spiritual harvest." Andrewes maintained that the Holy Spirit was actually sent fifty days after Easter so as to coincide with this "great feast under the law." Thus at Pentecost the "Law of Christ" supplanted the Old Law, and was "written in our hearts by the Holy Ghost."[249]

---

247. Ibid., p. 211.
248. This was delivered as part of the Metropolitan Ignatius of Latakia's address to the Assembly of the World Council of Churches at Uppsala in June 1968. M. Ramsay, *The Holy Spirit* (London, 1977). pp. 126 - 7.
249. Andrewes, Vol. 3, p. 111.

Under this New Covenant, Andrewes indicated, Christians received these "first fruits" firstly "in our Baptism, which is to us our 'laver of regeneration, and our renewing by the Holy Spirit.'" Nevertheless, we grow stale in our faithfulness and therefore we need a feast like Pentecost to re-consecrate our lives:

> It is with us, as with the fields, that we need a feast of first fruits, a day of consecration every year. By something or other we grow unhallowed, and need to be consecrated anew, to re-seize us of the first fruits of the Spirit again. That which was given us, and by the fraud of our enemy, or our own negligence, or both, taken from us and lost, we need to have restored; that which we have quenched, to be lit anew; that which we have cast into a dead sleep, awaken up from it. [250]

This re-consecration of our Christian lives at Pentecost, Andrewes suggested, should always be done in the context of the Eucharist:

> And if we ask, what shall be our means of this consecrating? [The writer to the Hebrews] telleth us, we are sanctified by the "oblation of the body of Jesus." That is the best means to restore us to that life. He has said it, and shewed it Himself; "He who eats Me will live by Me." The words spoken concerning that, are both "spirit and life".... Such was the means of our death, by eating the forbidden fruit, the first fruits of death; and such is the means of our life, by eating the flesh of Christ, the first fruits of life. [251]

"Thus when...we say *Accipite corpus*, we may safely say with the same breath *Accipite Spiritum*; and as truly every way. For that body is never without this Spirit." Andrewes believed that there was no better way to manifest this equality than by sending Christ "to the presence of the most holy mysteries." When Christ spoke in St. John's gospel "'if any thirst, let him come to Me and drink,'" he meant "of the Spirit." Hence Christ's "flesh and blood...are not spiritless...'His Spirit is with them' and makes them that 'meat that perisheth not, but endures to life everlasting.'" It is also the Holy

---

250. Ibid., Vol. 2, pp. 219-20.
251. Ibid., p. 220.

Spirit who gives unity to all who partake in the Sacrament. Here we all "drink of one Spirit, that there may be but one spirit in us."[252]

So it is obvious that the Holy Spirit can never be divorced from the sacraments; his Spirit is always present in them. The sacraments are "pledges of His love and favour, to our great and endless comfort." The "Comforter" which God sent to his Church on Pentecost "is Christ" in the Blessed Sacrament so that "by the flesh we eat, and the blood we drink at His table, we be made partakers of His Spirit, and of the comfort of it." [253]

Pentecost, like Spring, bestows gifts of many kinds, of which the most precious is new life, and through that life we can experience so many moments of sheer delight. It is his *"dies donorum....* Some gift He will give, either from the wind, inward, or from the tongue, outward." The most special of all His gifts is love, remarked Andrewes, and thus Pentecost should be known as the *festum charitatis*, when love itself is especially honored. Yet, if we are to be given this gift of love, then Love must dwell within. The Spirit is thus the "love-knot" that binds us to Christ and unites the Godhead. He "is the very essential unity, love and love-knot of the two persons, the Father and the Son; even of God with God." [254]

If we want to discover this love, Andrewes again directs us to the Sacrament:

> The undoubted both sign and means of His dwelling, what better way, or how sooner wrought, than by the sacrament of love, as the feast of love, upon the feast day of love; when love descended with both his hands full of gifts, for very love to take up His dwelling with us? ... He left us the gifts of His body and blood. His body broken, and full of the characters of love all over. His blood shed, every drop whereof is a great drop of love. To those which were sent, these which were left, love, joy, peace, have a special connatural reference, to breed and to maintain each other. His body the Spirit of strength, His blood the Spirit of comfort; both, the Spirit of love.

---

252.   Ibid., Vol. 3, pp.162, 179, 239, 278, 355.
253.   Ibid., p. 161.
254.   Ibid., pp. 113, 129.

After receiving the Sacrament, the Holy Spirit directs us to be united to one another in love:

> For here is "spiritual meat," that is breeding the Spirit; and here we are all made drink of one Spirit, that there may be but one spirit in us. And we are all made "one bread, and one body," kneaded together, and pressed together into one—as the symbols are, the bread, and the wine—so many as are partakers of one bread and one cup, "the bread of life," and "the cup of blessing," the communion of the Body and Blood of Christ.[255]

Once the Spirit implants himself within us, he will lead us to the "perfection of life to come"; that is, to where Christ has ascended.

> Will you now hear the end of all? By this means 'God will dwell with us'—the perfection of this life; and He dwelling with us, we shall dwell with Him—the last and the highest perfection of the life to come. For with whom God dwells here, they will dwell with Him there, certainly. Grace He does give, that He may 'dwell with us;' and glory He will give, that we may dwell with Him. So may He dwell, He with us: so may we dwell, we with Him, eternally.[256]

As we celebrate the Pentecost, we should keep in mind the following:

> Resolve then not to send Him away, on His own day, and nothing done, but to receive His seal, and to dispose ourselves, as pliable and fit to receive it. And that shall we but evil do, no not at all, unless it please Him to take us in hand and to work ready for it. To pray Him then so to do, to give us hearts of wax that will receive this impression; and having received it, to give us careful minds…to look at it, that it take as little harm as our infirmity will permit. That so we may keep ourselves from this unkind sin of grieving Him Who has been, and is, so good to us.[257]

---

255. Ibid., pp. 238 - 9.
256. Ibid., p.239.
257. Ibid., p. 20.

CHAPTER THIRTEEN
THE PERENNIAL PATH:
TOWARDS PERFECTION

The state of grace is the perfection of this life,
to grow still from grace to grace, to profit in it.
As to go on still forward is the perfection of
a traveller, to draw still nearer and nearer
to his journey's end. "To work today
and to-morrow as Christ said, and the
third day to be perfect, perfectly perfect."[258]

Much of Andrewes' preaching was directed towards the attaining of perfection and holiness in this life in preparation for the next. All this was now nearly possible through the Incarnation. He explained how the Hebrew word for "flesh" was the same as "for good tidings." This "good tidings" has now "come to pass" as "the Word is now become flesh." God was content to be born of "the woman's seed," that is, of the nature of man, in order to restore him to the perfection of that first paradise. This means that "He and we become not only 'one flesh,' as man and wife do by conjugal union, but even one blood too, as brethren by natural union." Thus the most wonderful feature of God taking our flesh is that through his Spirit we "are partakers of his Divine nature," and that "He might 'dwell in us and we in Him.'" Therefore we have the potential to perfection, in which, in its highest form, "we come near" to the likeness of "an angel."[259]

---

258. Ibid., p. 367.
259. Ibid., Vol. 1, pp. 4, 9, 16, 89.

Although Christians have that potential for perfection through Christ, they have to overcome the hindrance, the huge hindrance that prevents this—sin. "Unlesse we temper our affections we shall never be partakers of the divine nature"; for "when we commit sin, we die, we are dead in sin"; and any progress we have made in the Christian life is brought to a standstill. Andrewes therefore urged his contemporaries to quickly examine their actions, say "what have I done," and to be sorry for them "while they are fresh and newly committed." They must be able to say, humbly and sincerely as David did, "I have sinned and done wickedly." So we must repent quickly and often for our sins. Indeed, as Andrewes preached on Easter 1606, "Our lives become a cycle of sinning, repenting, confessing, and amendment. When we repent, we revive again; when we repent ourselves of our repenting and relapse back, then sin riseth again from the dead; and so *toties quoties*. And even upon these two, as two hinges, turneth our whole life. All our life is spent in one of them."[260]

Often, however, we forget the benefit of our contrition and cleansing, and the remembrance of our sins "soon departeth away." What we need to do, Andrewes suggested, is to follow the example of "the sinfull woman," who, "when she remembered that Christ had forgiven her many sinnes, was provoked thereby to love him much." We should also remember Paul, who was more than "carefull to walk in holiness of life" when he remembered that his sins were forgiven after his persecution of the Church of God.[261]

It is simply no good for us to believe that, as Christ has purged our sins, "we do not have to be careful of the holiness of life." The purpose of that purging is to allow us to follow a new life and be refreshed and renewed in Christ, but if we continually gloss over our sins, or ignore or make excuses for them, we shall never taste of eternal life. Thus "the end of our purging...is not to continue in sin, but, as Christ saith, 'I will refresh you, that you may take my yoke upon you, and be obedient unto me.'" (Mat. 11) [262]

It is "ceasing from sin [which] brings with it a good life, [and] that ever carries with it a good conscience." Actually, though, when

---

260. Ibid., Vol. 2, p. 202; *Apos. Sacra.*, pp. 548-9, 631.
261. Ibid, p. 549.
262. Ibid., p. 548.

Andrewes preached "to cease from sin" what he really meant was to cease "not from sin altogether—that is a higher perfection than this life will bear, but...from the 'dominion of sin.'" However, until we are free of "death itself, which in this life we are not, we shall not be free from sin altogether." One of the safeguards against the dominion of sin, he believed, was not to be an "idle Christian." "We must remember that many things and much time must be bestowed in seeking to garnish our souls" as we progress in overcoming the "dominion of sin." Hence Christ's way demands us to "labour" in "a new life" and with a "new conversation."[263]

Reading his *Preces* and sermons, it is obvious that Andrewes personally knew the pains of striving towards perfection. When he preached at St. Giles that "men must not persuade themselves it is an easie matter to be a good Christian," he was also addressing himself. It takes "all care and diligence...and the spirit of God to direct...in ceasing from evil and following good." Yet God knows of the conflict within us when "we cannot do what we would." Another example of this struggle is found in his 1610 Pentecost sermon: "For who can do this, keep the Commandments?" It is as impossible as it is "to fly or walk on the sea." Thus Andrewes' sermons unfolded his own spiritual journey with many confessions of failures, struggles with sin, the pain and joy of a penitent, and his longing for the final consummation with the glorified Christ. "That day will come...when...He will...take us to Himself. That as He hath been our *Emmanuel* upon earth, so He may be our *Emmanuel* in Heaven; He with us, and we with Him, there for ever."[264]

Accordingly, his sermons repeatedly manifested a longing to overcome all imperfections. This is clearly demonstrated in his 1606 Paschal sermon:

> [To] die and live as He did, that is "once for all"; which is an utter abandoning "once" of sin's dominion, and a continual, constant, persisting in a good course "once" begun. Sin's dominion, it languisheth sometimes in us, and falleth happily into a swoon, but it dies not quite "once for all." Grace lifteth up the eye, and looketh up a little, and giveth some sign of life, but never perfectly

---

263. Andrewes, Vol. 2, pp. 200; *Apos. Sacra*; p. 127, 154.
264. Ibid., p.625; Andrewes, Vol. 1, p. 152, Vol. 3, p. 151.

receiveth. O that once we might come to this! no more deaths, no more resurrections, but one! that we might once make an end of our daily continual [relapses] to which we are so subject, and once get past these pangs and qualms of godliness, this righteousness like the morning cloud, which is all we perform; that we might grow habituate in grace…"rooted and founded in it"; "steady" and "never to be removed"; that we might enter into, and pass a good account of this our *similiter et vos*![265]

Those early sermons on the Temptations of Christ, first published in 1592, also manifested that they were preached by one who struggled and fought with sin in his striving towards perfection. Yet we should not be discouraged, as Christ himself was sorely tempted, as well as the monks and hermits of the desert—despite their solitude. Indeed, we can learn from these holy men who were "content to creep on hands and feet to Him" in times of temptation. None can escape this struggle, as Andrewes intimated in one of his Genesis lectures: "Every Christian is…to strive against his own lusts, and to fight with sinne, which is the Serpents seed: There must be a bruising between the heel of the *Adams* seed and the Serpents head; this combat we must all undergoe." It is a combat lasting to the grave, but Christians are given a shield in Christ, especially in the Sacrament, against sin.[266]

Christians begin their covenantal relationship with God in Baptism when they are marked with the sign of the cross to fight against sin. Furthermore, Andrewes indicated, in Baptism "our souls are endued with inherent virtues, and receive grace and ability from God, to proceed from one degree of perfection to another all our life time, even till the time of our death, which is the beginning and accomplishment of our perfection." After Baptism in the other twin sacrament, the Eucharist, we are given support in the "accomplishment of perfection," as here we receive our Lord himself. We "are never so near Him, nor He us, as then and there." Therefore we must come often to the altar for "that blessed union [which] is the highest perfection we can in this life aspire unto." [267]

---

265. Ibid., Vol. 2, pp. 202 – 3.
266. Ibid., Vol. 5, p. 486; *Apos. Sacra.*, p. 406.
267. Andrewes, Vol. 1, p. 283, Vol. 2, p. 322, Vol. 5, p. 315.

Andrewes, in order to aid our reflection, compared this Blessed Sacrament to a tree; "Every tree must have a root," so Christ speaks of the Sacrament being a root when "it is sown in the hearts of the receivers." In time, through the working of the Holy Spirit, it "shoots forth and becomes a tree," giving "a life of grace" to fight against sin. In due time from this "life of grace" we shall receive, when our bodies are raised up from "the dust of death" to "the life of glory" in "the heavenly Paradise."[268]

Another suggestion by Andrewes for reflecting on our life towards perfection was to ponder on God's act of creation. All was perfect. Nowhere was perfection more manifest than in paradise, where God placed man for his eternal enjoyment and pleasure. Here were "herbs, flowers, plants and trees, of all sorts...speciall to that place alone."[269]

A further reflection is on repentance. Repentance must also bring forth fruit like the trees of summer. Therefore "we may not stand...about the tree, we are called on for *proferte*, to bring somewhat forth; else how shall we know it is a tree and no log? ... It is the bringing forth that makes the difference." Thus repentance has to lead to an amendment of life that gradually enables a Christian to grow in perfection—a life's work.[270]

Yet another reflection is our Lord's encounter with the Devil. If he had succumbed to him, Christ would have thwarted God's purpose, and so do we when we are lured by Satan to take the easy way. Andrewes illustrated this in his fourth Temptation sermon when he described the devil taking Christ up to the highest point in the mountain: "Whereas the ordinary way was down the stairs, he would have Him leap or throw Himself over the battlements." From this "a man may see to what end the devil's exalting cometh; he brings a man up by little and little to some high place, that so high may send him at once with his head down-ward. Yet all the preferments that he bestoweth on a man is not to any other intent but that he may do as the devil himself did." That is not the way towards perfection, but damnation. However, there were five "ordinary means" to prepare ourselves against the devil's temptations and

---

268.   *Apos. Sacra*, pp. 576 - 8.
269.   Ibid., pp. 107-8.
270.   Andrewes, Vol. 1, p. 438.

to grow towards perfection: using God's sacraments, meditating in a "solitary place...to kindle good thoughts," fasting, praying vigilantly, and "perfecting ourselves in the Scriptures." To seek in any other way is not God's. Undoubtedly for Andrewes one of the main functions of angels is their support of Christians in their daily warfare against the devil's temptations.[271]

The aim of all Andrewes' preaching was to lead his auditors to the beatific vision, a place of unspeakable joys where our corruptible bodies become incorruptible, and the faithful are united to Christ. This certainty made it possible, Andrewes believed, for all Christians to rise above all uncertainties and difficulties in this life.[272] That is why Andrewes always emphasised the importance of the "now" in the lives of Christians, and the need to pray continually for the Holy Spirit's dwelling. To live in a state of grace is essentially the gift of the Holy Spirit; it certainly is not "in the power of nature to elevate and lift itself up to conceive hope of being partakers of the blessedness of the life to come, to be made 'partakers of the Divine Nature,' and of the heavenly substance." It is only that divine gift of the Spirit, which makes "perfect which is imperfect," and enables us "to grow still from grace to grace." Andrewes believed such growth to be the goal of all Christians, for which they should be striving. By "growing from grace to grace" we are transported from one "'fulness...to be partakers of another...the fulness of eternity." Here we shall be blessed with grace through the Holy Spirit to "receive the fulness of our redemption...and the full fruit of [our] inheritance." "Then it will be perfect, complete, absolute fulness indeed, when we shall all be filled with 'the fulness of Him that filleth all in all.'"[273]

So until the grave we must persevere in the path to perfection. As St. Gregory said, "Of all Virtues only Perseverance is crowned." "We receive grace to proceed from one degree of perfection to another all our lives." We must recognise "to go on still forward is the perfection of a traveller," and "to grow still from grace to grace" until our lives' end.[274]

---

271. Ibid., Vol. 5, pp. 503 – 4, 520.

272. Ms. 3707, p. 109.

273. Andrewes, Vol. 1, p. 63, Vol. 3, p. 367; Vol. 5, pp. 306, 315.

274. Andrewes, Vol. 3, p. 367; *Apos. Sacra*, p. 124.

CHAPTER FOURTEEN
THE PERENNIAL FAITH: DOCTRINE

*I yeeld upp into the hands of Allmightie God that which
he hath created, that which he hath redeemed, that
which he hath regenerated, most humbly beseeching him
to make mee partaker by the mercies of the Father, and
through the meritts of his Sonne, of the forgiveness of my Sinnes,
and all the comforts of his Holy Spirit pertayning to his
covenant made with mankind in the death of his Sonne.*[275]

Andrewes was not an original theologian—that would have
been contrary to his own belief that the Church's doctrine had
already been formulated and well taught by the Fathers. His duty
was to continue in their footsteps and instruct his students and
other contemporaries in the ancient Catholic faith. The refrain in
Faith of our Fathers encapsulates Andrewes' sentiment:

Faith of our fathers, holy faith!
We will be true to thee till death.[276]

When we peruse his sermons we discover comments that make
manifest his commitment to the Fathers:

And may not the same in like reason be said and entreated at this
day? That what our Fathers and Elders in the Christian Faith

---

275.   Ibid., Vol. 11, p. c. This was the preamble to Andrewes' will.
276.   W. Faber, in *The Breaking of Bread* (Oregon, 2000), hymn no. 447.

bounteously employed on Christ; what they, I say, have that way dedicate, if we will not add to it and imitate them, yet we will let it alone and not trouble them.[277]

For Andrewes, like the Eastern Fathers, the basic faith is an expression of beliefs rather than a tool for speculation—as often happened in many of the Western Schools. He insisted that there should always be a shroud of mystery about God, as we humans are not meant to comprehend everything—that would make us equal to God. The two great mysteries of the Catholic Faith, and therefore for Andrewes, were the Incarnation and the Trinity. No mind could ever understand logically how the Word could leave Heaven, come down to earth to be born as we are, and wear our rags. We must ponder on the great humiliation of God (kenosis) to be made one of us, and marvel in it and what it has done for us.

> This great God who measureth the earth [Hab. 3:6] and sea, the sun, moon and starrs; who sustaines all things created, governs them without pain or wearinesse, in so much that a leafe from a tree cannot fall to the ground without him. This is he who made hims[elf] of so small reputacion as to be made in the likenes of man.[278]

Likewise, the doctrine of the Trinity is even more complex. He believed that no analogy could adequately explain this, even though he tried by using light and running water. The sun "begetteth his own Beames and from thence proceedeth light, and yet is none of them before another," all give light, whilst with water "there is the well head, the spring boiling out of it, and the stream flowing from them both, and all these are but one water."[279]

Whatever we need to know about the Catholic Faith can all be found in Andrewes' sermons and lectures. His Court sermons concentrate on the Incarnation and its implication for all mankind and creation, as well as the work of the Holy Spirit in this world and in the lives of Christians. These and other sermons also taught on the necessity of believing in the Sacraments to be a Christian.

---

277.   Andrewes, Vol. 2, p. 49.
278.   Ms. 3707, p. 137.
279.   Ibid., p. 56.

So if Andrewes were to instruct us today on how we become a Christian, what we must believe to be a Christian, and what is necessary to be a faithful Christian, what would he tell us?

For Andrewes, the only way to become a Christian is through the sacrament of Baptism. Here in this sacrament we, or our Godparents on our behalf, make promises and declare our belief in the Christian creed. Baptism and the Eucharist are both necessary for salvation, and both of these are intricately linked with Christ's death on the cross.

Thus church membership could never be separated from Christ's sacrifice on Calvary, from whence flowed water and blood. That water initiates Christians into his death, whilst his blood "hath redeemed us to be 'a peculiar people.'" As Christ is the Head of the Church, the baptised are therefore "His Church" and members of "His Kingdom by right of purchase." Baptism is hence the sacrament of initiation into life eternal. "For Heaven-gate...doth ever open at baptism; In sign, he that new cometh from the font, hath then the right of entrance in thither." Once baptised "we carry His name, for as He is Christ, so we are of Him called Christians." It is also the Christian's Passover as it symbolises the "great change" when the baptised are delivered from bondage to freedom, and from mortality to immortality. [280]

Baptism, for Andrewes, is also the beginning of a Christian's covenantal relationship with God. It is also the beginning of a Christian's growth towards perfection. Through Baptism "our souls are endued with inherent virtues, and receive grace and ability from God, to proceed from one degree of perfection to another all our life time, even till the time of our death, which is the beginning and accomplishment of our perfection."[281]

After we are baptised we sin and break our contract with God. However, this can be renewed constantly in the Eucharist when we receive the Sacrament and are united with our blessed Saviour. Andrewes stressed that the Sacrament is not only the heart of Christian worship but is also the centre of the Scriptures, uniting the Old and the New Testaments. He illustrated this in his 1611 Paschal sermon with its theme of Christ as the Corner-stone: "'[W]hen

---

280.   Andrewes, Vol. 2, p. 372, Vol. 3, pp. 250, 258, 309, Vol. 5, p. 462.
281.   Ibid., Vol. 5, p. 315.

He joined the Lamb of the Passover and the Bread of the Eucharist', ending the one and beginning the other, recapitulating both Lamb and Bread into himself." This then makes "that Sacrament, by the very institution of it, to be as it were the very corner-stone of both the Testaments," and "the corner-stone of the Law and the Gospel."[282]

The celebration of the Eucharist is also where Heaven and earth meet. "For as there is a recapitulation of all in Heaven and earth in Christ, so there is a recapitulation of all in the holy Sacrament. You may see it clearly: there is in Christ the Word eternal for things in Heaven; there is also flesh for things on earth."[283]

The other sacrament that Andrewes emphasised as important in the life of a Christian is the sacrament of Penance, or Confession. This is because sin is our deadly enemy, and if we do not repent and confess then we are damned. Adam sinned for a "trifle," as we all do daily. "We are all to pray to God to take from us the opportunity of sinning; so frail we are, it is no sooner offered but we are ready to embrace it."[284] When we sin we should confess it, as is evident not only in Andrewes' sermons but also in his Visitation Articles. The latter inquired:

> Whether doth your Minister before the severall times of the administration of the Lords Supper, admonish and exhort his Parishioners, if they have their consciences troubled and disquieted, to resort unto him, or some other learned Minister, and open his grief, that he may receive such ghostly counsell and comfort, as his conscience may be relieved, and by the minister he may receive the benefit of absolution, to the quiet of his conscience.[285]

Andrewes' Prayer Book notes also stressed the importance of the priest reading the second exhortation to his people at the Eucharist, so that they could understand the gravity of sin and the benefit received from using the sacrament of confession: "It is most expedient that this be read to induce the people that they bethink

---

282. Ibid., Vol. 2, p. 288.
283. Ibid., Vol. 1, p. 281.
284. Ibid., Vol. 4, p. 159.
285. Ibid., Vol. 11, p. 131.

themselves of the absolute benefitt of absolution by their penitent confession."[286]

His Ash Wednesday sermons were full of reminders that Lent is a penitential season, and that Christians should follow the "discipline of repentance" of the early Christians, who during Lent were "open penitents in public" but for us now "in private." The true penitent will "confess humbly his sins before Thee, and...crave pardon for them" and be thankful that God opened his eyes to sin. Andrewes always maintained that "it is a perfect signe of an humble and a good mind, when one can say from his heart, let me bear the shame and punishment of my sinne."[287]

His sermon at Whitehall in 1600 was based on those words from St. John's Gospel of the first Easter day, "Whose soever sins ye remit...." He explained that "the remission of sins is an article of faith, no less than the resurrection of the body," because being absolved from sin is "in very deed a resurrection. By confessing our sins we are delivered from a "disease" and healed once more. [288]

The heart of the Gospel is the Incarnation and forgiveness, and Andrewes certainly preached this to us. They are God's gift to all mankind, irrespective of status in life. As Christ was born humbly, even the poorest of creatures know he is their Saviour, as illustrated in the shepherds coming to the stable: "But this is a sign for you— you that keep sheep, and such other poor people; you have a Saviour too. He is not the Saviour of great states only, but even of poor shepherds. The poorest of the earth may repair to Him."[289]

We must have the correct belief about Christ, insisted Andrewes. We simply cannot believe anything, and that is why the early church Councils set down what Christians must believe about Jesus Christ. The most important belief is that he is both divine and human—what theologians call the hypostatical union. Andrewes illustrated this at Christmass, 1610, by combining those words associated with Christ's birth:

---

286. Ibid., p. 155.
287. Ibid., Vol. 1, p. 393; *Apos. Sacra*, pp. 302, 312.
288. Andrewes, Vol. 5, pp. 83-5.
289. Ibid., Vol. 1, p. 201.

And now if we will put together *natus* and *Servator*, *Servator* and *Christus*, *Christus* and *Dominus*, *Dominus* and *natus*, "born and Saviour, Saviour and Christ, Christ and the Lord, the Lord and born"; take them which way you will in combination, any of the four, then have we His two natures in one Person. In *Servator*, His Godhead; none but God is a Saviour. In *Christus*, His Manhood; God cannot be anointed, man may. In *Dominus*, His Divine again, "the Lord from Heaven." In *Natus*, His human nature directly, born of a woman, both ever carefully joined, and to be joined together.

Of course, this is what St. John proclaimed in the beginning of his gospel: "*Verbum*, 'the Word,' there *Dominus*; and *caro*, 'the flesh,' that is *natus*."[290]

The shadow of the cross hovered above the Christ Child even in his cradle; it would remain ever with him—a shadow for much of his life, but a reality when his ministry gathered momentum. Our Lord gave his life as a ransom for mankind. Everything that our Lord suffered was for us. His death therefore not only paid "our debt", but also "bought for us...an everlasting inheritance and brought us to it.... All He did, all He suffered, all He bequeathed, all He was, He was for us." Thus:

> His thirsting on the crosse was not for water, he is the well of life, but for man's Redemption; his riseing from the dead, was not for hims[elf]; for so there was no more need of taking up his life, than of laying it down, but 'twas for us men, that we might be freed from the power of the grave.[291]

Calvary, for Andrewes—as well as the Cappadocian Fathers and the whole Orthodox tradition—could never be separated from the event in the Easter garden. "Christ's dying, and His rising are so linked together, and their audits so entangle one with another, as it is very hard to sever them." Redemption meant triumph over death, the penalty for Adam's sin. Death now becomes not something to be feared, but something to be anticipated with hope and joy.[292]

---

290. Ibid., p. 80.
291. Ibid., Vol. 3, p. 93; Ms. 3707, p. 148.
292. Meyendorff, op. cit., p. 162l; Andrewes, Vol. 2, p. 195.

Christ's victory over death means that our bodies too will be refined. After his "resurrection tho' his body was refined from all corruptible qualities, yet it remained still a true Humane body; his humane nature was then beautified with glory, but not abolished or annihilated." In like manner our bodies will rise at the last day, as expressed "in our Office of the Dead." Hence our resurrection and that of Christ's are closely bound.[293]

Although in the Resurrection all "good is revived" and made "anew," and "the hope of that life immortal is the very life of this life mortal," it still did not complete man's redemption. Just as Christ's death was entwined with the Resurrection, so the latter could never be seen as a *fait accompli* without the Ascension.

After all, what message of hope is it to souls to be told of a "rising" unless it leads to life, life eternal? "*Resurrexit*, tell that to all the world. All that die in Adam will rise in Christ—miscreants, Jews, Turks and all—no Gospel that, properly. Tell the Christian of more than so; tell him of *ascendo* too…that pertains to it." Indeed it is "better lie still in our graves, better never rise, than rise and rising not to ascend." Therefore we must set our minds on "*Ascendo*, look well to that as that completes Christ's redemptive work."[294]

During the Ascension, Christ took his manhood to Heaven, where he now performs his heavenly functions. As our High Priest he is our mediator to the Father. In view of some mediæval teachings, Andrewes stressed that Christ alone is our mediator: "He stands as a Mediator between the punishment and us, and hath shed his blood as a ransome for our sinnes…and for the reward which we should have deserved *fac hoc & vives*; howsoever we have debarred our selves from it."

Thus the end that Christ "aimed at in all his sorrowes and sufferings, victory and triumph [was for] the good of us men and for our salvacion." [295]

Before ascending, Our Lord promised to send the Holy Spirit to lead his Church. Andrewes followed the Western rather than the Eastern tradition in his teaching about the "procession" of the Holy Spirit; that is, the Holy Spirit proceeds "from the Father through

293.   Ibid., p. 261; Ms. 3707, p. 172.
294.   Andrewes, Vol. 2, p. 374, Vol. 3, pp. 45 - 7.
295.   *Apos. Sacra*, p. 571; Ms. 3707, p. 148.

the Son." Hence in his 1612 Whitsun sermon he stated that the Holy Spirit:

> Proceeds, and from both. 1. From the Father, the Constantinopolitan Council, from the express words, "Who proceedeth from the Father" (John 15:26); 2. From the Son; the Council of Toledo, the eighth, from the visible sign, where the Son breathed on the Apostles, and willed them from Him to "receive the Holy Ghost" (John 20:22). And, *Non a Semet Ipso loquetur, sed de Meo accipet* (John 16:13-14) sheweth fully as much.

To summarize, the Spirit is "sent by the Father *Filioque*, and by the Son too (John 14:26,15:26). And so, 'Spirit of the Father' (Mat. 10:20), *Filiique*, and 'of the Son' (Gal.4:6) too." [296]

I do not think, however, that Andrewes would insist that we have to accept the *Filoque clause*, as it became known, for salvation; rather, we must believe in the power and presence of the Holy Spirit to change and direct our lives, "but specially of the spiritual life which we seek for."[297]

Andrewes also taught that it was the Holy Spirit poured out on the Church at Pentecost that binds all the Christian feasts, beginning with the Annunciation, "when He descended on the Blessed Virgin, whereby the Son of God did take our nature, the nature of man. And in the Holy Ghost's coming they end, even in His descending this day upon the sons of men, whereby they actually become 'partakers of His nature, the nature of God.'"[298]

The recognition of angels and saints in the lives of Christians was also important to Andrewes. In his Michaelmas sermon in 1599 Andrewes expressed his view on the Christian attitude on angels. What he recommended was this: although "we doe not adore them with divine honour," we nevertheless have a "duty" to thank God for the benefits we receive from them. One of the benefits is that they continually leave God's presence, which "*is the fulnesse of all joy*" for them, and come down to earth to minister to our "vile bodies," "to take charge of us and keep us from danger." So we should thank God for having "created and commanded such excellent spir-

---

296. Andrewes, Vol. 3, pp. 188 - 9.
297. Ibid., Vol. 2, p. 219.
298. Ibid., Vol. 3, p. 146.

its to fight for us," and "pray that they which have thus fought for us in Heaven, may in earth fight with us to help us; that as they have cast him [the devil] out of Heaven, so we may overcome him in earth...and...drive the Dragon into the bottomlesse pit." Thus the angels support us in our daily warfare against the devil's temptations as we strive towards perfection. We also should "take heed that we provoke not the Angels with our misdeeds...nor alienate them from us with the wicked words of our mouths." We especially must remember not to offend nor alienate them by acts of irreverence at our worship in church. If we want their affection and their "care for our safeguard" we shall humbly cast ourselves before God in worship as the angelic host does.[299]

The saints are members of the Church Triumphant, as they have already run the race and won the prize long ago. Now they "look on us [and]...how well we carry ourselves." We in turn should "look to them, that we may carry ourselves well in the course we have undertaken." The saints, stated Andrewes, are therefore an inspiration for us to follow and imitate. Their fervency for prayers is our comfort and strength, for when "we pray but faintly and have not that supply of fervency that is required in prayer," we know that "God's saints...pray for us with all instancy." [300]

Andrewes taught that Eschatology, the doctrine of the four last things—death, judgment, Hell, and Heaven, is a part of our faith that we should ponder every day of our lives. Andrewes' message for us is that we should live as if each day is our last, and we should be conscious of the "eternal now"—we could die at this very moment. Then, for the faithful Christian, "death itself is nothing else but the very separation of the life from the body." This death is not "like a fall," not "like that of Pharaoh into the sea, that 'sunk down like a lump of lead' into the bottom, and never came up more; but a fall like that of Jonas into the sea, who was received by a fish, and after cast up again." The latter was but a foreshadowing of Christ's death, showing that his burial was not like that of "a log or stone" that "lieth still" in the ground, but like that "of a wheat-corn...which is quickened and springeth up again." Their bodies will be raised at the general Resurrection.[301]

---

299. *Apos.* Sacra., pp. 586, 593 - 4.
300. Andrewes, Vol. 5, p. 339.
301. Ibid.,Vol. 2, pp. 192-3.

To any who question the state of the resurrected body—especially if we should die with a weak, diseased body—Andrewes responded that we shall "rise with a glorious body, as free from diseases and corruption as the soul." It may have been "sown in weakenesse, dishonoured and mortality, [but] it shall be raised in Power and honour and to Immortality."[302]

As well as physical or corporal death when the body is laid in the grave, Andrewes also reminded us there were two other kinds of death: spiritual and eternal. Many live their whole lives spiritually dead, as they live without God. These have separated themselves "from the blessed communion" and have banished themselves "from the gracious presence of God" both now and in eternity. Those with deadened soul have a "totall deprivacion of primitive integrity and originall righteousnes" and "of sanctifying and saveing graces wherewith he was endured with in his creacion." Eternal death materialises on that day when the trumpet will sound and those who have denied God on this earth will be denied "the presence of God" and will live in "Hell, the place, the prison of the damned, where they shall suffer an insufferable and eternall punishment."[303]

None of us can escape Judgment. On that day, the second coming of Christ, we shall have to look at our Judge "upon His throne, in the end of the world." Andrewes told his contemporaries, and so he tells us: "Mark it well!" It is only the Spirit that can "save the flesh, by spiritualizing it; not the flesh destroy[ing] the Spirit, by carnalizing it; not the flesh weigh[ing] down the Spirit to earth hither, but the Spirit lift[ing] up the flesh thither to Heaven whence it came." We should "remember the fire, the thirst, and the torments" and learn from Lazarus' experience. What use is it to "never 'lift up our eyes' till we be 'in hell,' nor remember that may do us good till it be too late." "Remember...our being remembered" by Christ hinges on our "remembrance here." Nothing is more certain than that "he commeth to judge the world in truth." Henceforth we should "mend our lives, and then we shall rejoice and wish for his comming."[304]

---

302. Ms. 3707, p. 150.
303. Ibid., pp. 88-9.
304. Andrewes, Vol. 2, p. 96, Vol. 3, p. 311.

Andrewes emphasised that the difference between sinners in Heaven and sinners in Hell is that the latter never brought forth any fruits in their lives. Their tree, like that in the gospel, always remained barren, and upon Judgment it will not escape the axe. They will spend eternity in Hell in "eternall punishment," devoid of any comfort.[305]

However, those who have lived by the fruits of repentance will on that last day be called home to Heaven. At the general resurrection "these thick clods of earth shall be made glittering and glorious like so many starres of light," and thus our "earthly bodies shall become spirituall bodies and these weake ignorant soules, perfectly wise, just and holy like the Angells themselves." There in Heaven the faithful, resurrected to a life "of blisse and glory," can triumphantly sing "Death is swallowed up in victory." For Andrewes Heaven is a river of pleasure, "never ebbing, but ever flowing to all contentment," where the Logos, not only as the Son of God but also as the Son of man, welcomes us "in the life to come." Here we shall take "full possession of His own and His Father's bliss and happiness...which is the...highest pitch of all our hope." [306]

As "we are citizens of heaven" by virtue of our baptism, we should live by "the laws of our country" daily, which pleases "our heavenly Father." Ideally, this means continually lifting "up our hearts and affections from earth to heaven." Although we often fail, Andrewes stressed that by persevering and "growing from grace to grace...we shall come to be partakers of...the fulness of eternity...[and] receive the full fruition of the inheritance whereto we are but adopted." This "will be perfect, complete, absolute fulness indeed, when we shall all be filled with 'the fulness of Him that filleth all in all.'" It is "to this we aspire, and to this in the fulness appointed of every one of our times Almighty God bring us by Him, and for His sake, Who in this 'fulness of time' was sent to work it for us in His Person; and work it in us by the operation of His blessed Spirit."[307]

---

305. Ms.3707, p.89.
306. Ibid., p. 152; Andrewes, Vol.2, p. 198.
307. Ms. 3707, p. 63, Vol. 5, p. 379.

BIBLIOGRAPHY

ANDREWES, L. *Apospasmatia Sacra* (London, 1657).
The Works of Lancelot Andrewes, 11 vols
(Library of Anglo-Catholic Theology,
Oxford, 1841–1854).
The Morall Law Expounded (London,
1642).
*Scala Coeli: Nineteene Sermons Concerning
Prayer* (London, 1611).

BETTENSEN, H. (Ed.) *The Later Christian Fathers* (Oxford,
1989).

BRIGHTMAN, F. E. *The Private Devotions of Lancelot Andrewes*
(Gloucester, Mass, Ed. & Trans., 1978).

BROOKES, P. *New English Hymnal* (Canterbury Press,
Norwich, 1988).

CHRYSOSTOM *The Nicene and Post-Nicene Fathers*, 1st
series, Vol. 10 (Edinburgh, 1991).

CHURCH, R. W. *Paschal and other Sermons* (London, 1895).

CYPRIAN *The Epistles Of S. Cyprian*, Library of the
Fathers, Vol. 17 (Oxford: J. H. Parker,
1844).

DUFFY, E.   *The Stripping of the Altars, Traditional Religion in England 1440–1580*, (Yale, 1993).

ELIOT, T. S.   *For Lancelot Andrewes: Essays on Style and Order* (1928).
                      Selected Poems (London, 1980).

FABER, W.   *Faith of our Fathers* in *The Breaking of Bread* (Oregon, 2000).

HOPKINS, G. M.   *The Poetical Works of Gerard Manley Hopkins*, ed. R. Bridges (London, 1918).

ISSACSON, H.   *Institutiones Piae* (London, 1630).

KEBLE, J.   *The Christian Year*, (Oxford, 1827).

MEYENDORFF, J.   *Byzantium Theology* (New York, 1983).

OMAN, C.C.   *English Church Plate*, (London, 1957).

RAMSAY, M.   *The Holy Spirit* (London, 1977).

USSHER, R. G.   *The Presbyterian Movement in the Reign of Queen Elizabeth as Illustrated by the Minute Book of the Dedham Classis 1582 - 1589*, Camden Society, 3rd Series, Vol. 8 (London, 1905).

WELSBY, P.   *Lancelot Andrewes* (London, 1958).

WILLIAMS, O. (Ed.)   *The Mentor of Major British Poets* (New York, 1963).

Manuscript   Lambeth Palace Ms. 3707.

Printed in the United States
58055LVS00002B/43